hamlyn cookery club

Quick
cooking

hamlyn cookery club

Quick
cooking

First published in 1999 by Hamlyn
an imprint of Octopus Publishing Group Ltd
2–4 Heron Quays
London E14 4JP

British Library Cataloguing-in-Publication Data
A catalogue record for this book is available from the
British Library.

ISBN 0 600 59917 5

Printed in China

Publishing Director: Laura Bamford
Copy Editor: Linda Doeser
Creative Director: Keith Martin
Design Manager: Bryan Dunn
Designer: Martin Topping
Jacket Photography: Sean Myers
Picture Researcher: Christine Junemann
Senior Production Controller: Katherine Hockley

Notes

1 Both metric and imperial measurements have been given in
all recipes. Use one set of measurements only and not a
mixture of both.

2 Standard level spoon measurements are used in all recipes.
1 tablespoon = one 15 ml spoon
1 teaspoon = one 5 ml spoon

3 Eggs should be medium unless otherwise stated. The
Department of Health advises that eggs should not be
consumed raw. This book may contain dishes made with
raw or lightly cooked eggs. It is prudent for more
vulnerable people such as pregnant or nursing mothers,
the elderly, babies and young children to avoid these
dishes. Once prepared, these dishes should be refrigerated
and eaten promptly.

4 Milk should be full fat unless otherwise stated.

5 Fresh herbs should be used unless otherwise stated.
If unavailable use dried herbs as an alternative but halve the
quantities stated.

6 Pepper should be freshly ground black pepper unless
otherwise stated.

7 Ovens should be preheated to the specified temperature
– if using a fan-assisted oven, follow the manufacturer's
instructions for adjusting the time and temperature.

8 Measurements for canned food have been given as a
standard metric equivalent.

Contents

Introduction

Just because the pace of life these days verges on the frantic, it doesn't mean that you have to sacrifice good food and the pleasure of family mealtimes. No one wants to slave over a hot stove after a hard day's work, but fast food doesn't have to mean junk food. All the dishes in this book can be prepared and cooked within 30 minutes – some in far less time – and are both tasty and nourishing.

There are recipes for all family occasions, every course and any time of year and many can be adapted for instant entertaining. Midweek meals have never been easier, whether you want a light snack, a substantial curry, a summery salad or a vegetarian bake. For those with a sweet tooth, but no time, the quick and easy desserts are a dream come true.

Planning Ahead

It is worth taking a few minutes for planning the week's menus, so that when the time comes to cook, everything runs smoothly and easily. What is more, you then won't have to spend every lunchtime racing around the nearest supermarket. There are other practical ways to make life simpler, too. While there is nothing like home-cooked food, clever use of adaptable ready-prepared products saves time and effort. Condensed soups combined with fresh vegetables or herbs form a good basis for a sauce, instant mashed potato is an easy and attractive topping for all kinds of bakes and frozen pastry is ideal for both savoury and sweet dishes.

If you are very well organized, you can take advantage of these speedy recipes by preparing double the quantity, which, fortunately, won't take twice the time. Freeze the extra and then later on, you can give yourself an evening off in the knowledge that a home-cooked meal is already prepared. People who are good at time management can split some recipes over two evenings, carrying out the first part of the preparation the night before cooking the dish. This allows extra time for meat to marinate or desserts to chill.

Canned Goods

Cans of peeled plum tomatoes, both whole and chopped, are time-savers for sauces, soups and casseroles. There are also now chopped tomatoes available ready flavoured with various herbs and garlic. Cans of tuna can turn a salad into a main meal or make a delicious sauce for pasta or rice. Canned beans such as kidney beans can be used in salads, and added to sauces for pasta and rice.

Dry Goods

Pasta has to be one of the most versatile and quick foods available, use different shapes to ring the changes. Fresh pasta is even quicker to cook than dried. Rice is also extremely quick to cook; try Basmati, Arborio and long-grain.

Frozen Foods

Use quick thawing fruits such as raspberries, blackcurrants and bilberries in a dessert or purée them to make quick sauces. Ice cream, both vanilla and flavoured, means you are never without a dessert. Keep a store of ready-made shortcrust and puff pastry in the freezer as well as some ready baked pastry cases in different sizes.

Finding a Dish for any Occasion

The recipes in this book have been divided into five chapters: Suppers and Snacks, Main Courses, Vegetarian, Vegetables and Salads, and Desserts. This makes it easy to find exactly the right dish to suit the occasion, the time available, personal tastes and the family budget, but there is no need to be rigid. Serve home-made soup with fresh crusty bread and, perhaps, a special cheese and you have a filling main course. Many of the vegetable dishes and salads work just as well as starters as they do as accompaniments. Meat-eaters will enjoy a vegetarian main course for a change. Feel free to experiment with ingredients, too, substituting seasonal vegetables, for example.

Quick Cooking ensures that cooking is a pleasure, not a chore, even when time is short, and that midweek meals are delicious, nutritious and a pleasure both to serve and eat.

Suppers and Snacks

Sweet Pepper Soup

40 g (1½ oz) butter

1 large onion, finely chopped

1 garlic clove, crushed

25 g (1 oz) plain flour

900 ml (1½ pints) chicken stock

500 g (1 lb) red peppers, cored,
deseeded and chopped

1 dried red chilli, chopped

250 g (8 oz) tomatoes, skinned,
deseeded and chopped

1 teaspoon chopped thyme

chopped chives, to garnish

Melt the butter in a large pan. Add the onion and garlic and fry gently for 2 minutes. Stir in the flour and cook for a further 2 minutes.

Gradually add the stock, stirring constantly, and bring to the boil.

Add the red peppers, chilli, tomatoes and thyme. Cover and simmer for 15–20 minutes, until the vegetables are tender. Cool slightly.

Sieve or process in a blender or food processor until smooth. Return to the pan and heat through. Garnish with chives before serving.

Serves 6

right (clockwise from left): sweet pepper soup; garlic soup; aubergine and crab soup

Garlic Soup

2 tablespoons olive oil

24 garlic cloves, peeled

900 ml (1½ pints) beef or chicken
stock

1 bouquet garni

pinch of grated nutmeg

1 blade mace

3 egg yolks

6–8 slices bread

salt and pepper

chopped parsley, to garnish

grated Parmesan cheese, to serve

Heat the oil in a large pan. Add the whole garlic cloves and fry, without browning, for 5 minutes.

Stir in the stock and add the bouquet garni, nutmeg and mace and season with salt and pepper to taste. Bring to the boil, cover and simmer for 20 minutes.

Blend the egg yolks with 2 tablespoons of the soup. Strain the remaining soup and return to the pan. Bring to the boil, then remove from the heat.

Meanwhile, toast the bread on both sides and place in individual soup bowls.

Pour the egg mixture into the soup, stirring well. Ladle into the bowls, garnish with parsley and serve with the Parmesan.

Serves 6–8

Aubergine and Crab Soup

1 tablespoon vegetable oil

2 large onions, chopped

2 garlic cloves, crushed

4 large aubergines, peeled and
chopped

1 x 400 g (13 oz) can tomatoes

300 ml (½ pint) chicken stock

1 tablespoon tomato purée

1 bouquet garni

125 ml (4 fl oz) dry white wine

175 g (6 oz) can crabmeat, drained

salt and pepper

chopped parsley, to garnish

Heat the oil in a pan. Add the onions and garlic and cook for 5 minutes, without browning. Stir in the aubergines and the tomatoes with their juice.

Bring to the boil over a low heat and stir in the stock, tomato purée, bouquet garni and wine. Season to taste. Cover and simmer for about 20 minutes, until the vegetables are tender. Remove and discard the bouquet garni and cool slightly.

Sieve or process in a blender until smooth. Return to the pan. Flake and stir in the crabmeat and bring to the boil. Serve immediately, garnished with chopped parsley.

Serves 6

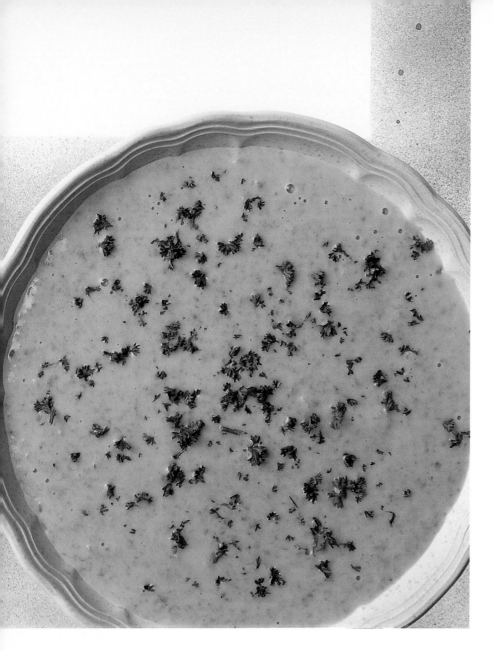

Rösti

1 kg (2 lb) even-sized potatoes,
  scrubbed but not peeled
1 small onion, finely chopped
50 g (2 oz) butter
salt and pepper

Cook the potatoes in a saucepan of boiling salted water for 8 minutes, but do not over-cook. Drain well and return to the pan. Place over a moderate heat for a few seconds, shaking the pan frequently. Remove from the heat and leave to cool.

Peel the potatoes and grate them coarsely into a bowl. Add the onion and season to taste with salt and pepper. Stir well to mix.

Melt the butter in a heavy-based frying pan, add the potato mixture and fry over a moderate heat for about 8 minutes, turning the mixture occasionally, until lightly golden on the underside. Pat down gently to form a neat cake covering the base of the pan. Cook for a further 10 minutes until golden brown on the underside.

Loosen with a palette knife and invert on to a hot serving plate. Cut into wedges and serve at once.

Serves 6

Note: The potatoes can be cooked a day ahead, then stored in a cool place. This Swiss potato dish is delicious served on its own or as an accompaniment to grilled or roast meat, sausages, or bacon and eggs.

Mushroom Soup with Madeira

75 g (3 oz) butter
1 large onion, finely chopped
500 g (1 lb) mushrooms, finely
  chopped
25 g (1 oz) plain flour
900 ml (1½ pints) chicken stock
125 ml (4 fl oz) dry Madeira
150 ml (¼ pint) double cream
salt and pepper
chopped parsley, to garnish

Melt the butter in a large pan. Add the onion and cook for 20 minutes or until evenly browned. Add the mushrooms and cook for 2 minutes.

Stir in the flour and cook for 1 minute. Gradually stir in the stock, then season with salt and pepper to taste. Bring to the boil, cover and simmer for 10 minutes.

Stir in the Madeira and double cream and heat through gently. Stir and serve immediately, garnished with parsley.

Serves 4–6

Tomato and Cheese Soup

25 g (1 oz) butter

2 large onions, chopped

25 g (1 oz) plain flour

1 kg (2 lb) tomatoes, skinned,
  deseeded and chopped

1 garlic clove, crushed

1 sprig of rosemary

1 sprig of thyme

600 ml (1 pint) chicken stock

150 ml (¼ pint) double cream

1 egg yolk

125 g (4 oz) Gruyère cheese, grated

salt and pepper

Melt the butter gently in a pan. Add the onions and cook over a low heat, without browning, for about 5–6 minutes. Stir in the flour and cook for 1 further minute. Stir in the tomatoes, garlic, herbs, stock and season to taste.

Bring to the boil, cover and simmer for 20 minutes, or until the tomatoes are very tender. Cool slightly, then sieve or process in a blender or food processor until smooth. Return to the pan.

Blend the cream and egg yolk together and stir into the pan. Heat through gently; do not boil or the soup will curdle. Stir in the Gruyère and serve immediately.

Serves 6–8

left: mushroom soup with madeira;
right: tomato and cheese soup

Savoury Onion Puffs

25 g (1 oz) butter
375 g (12 oz) onions, chopped
175 g (6 oz) potatoes, boiled and diced
300 ml (½ pint) packet onion sauce mix
200 ml (7 fl oz) milk
125 g (4 oz) Cheddar cheese, grated
250 g (8 oz) puff pastry, defrosted, if frozen
beaten egg, to glaze
salt and pepper

Melt the butter in a pan. Add the onions and cook over a low heat for 5 minutes. Add the potatoes.

Make up the sauce mix with the milk, as directed on the packet. Stir into the onion mixture with the Cheddar and season with salt and pepper to taste. Cook for 3 minutes.

Roll out the pastry on a lightly floured board to a 30 cm (12 inch) square and cut into 4 squares. Place on a baking sheet.

Place one-quarter of the onion mixture in the centre of each square. Dampen the edges and fold the pastry over the filling to form triangular puffs. Seal the edges, trim, knock up and flute. Brush the pastry with beaten egg.

Cook in a preheated oven, 220°C (425°F), Gas Mark 7, for 15 minutes until well risen and golden.

Serves 4

Tomato Fondue

50 g (2 oz) butter
1 small onion, finely chopped
2 garlic cloves, crushed
2 x 400 g (13 oz) cans tomatoes
1 teaspoon dried oregano
1 teaspoon paprika
2 teaspoons dried basil
300 ml (½ pint) dry white wine
500 g (1 lb) Cheddar cheese, grated
salt and pepper
bread cubes, to serve

Melt the butter in a fondue dish or flameproof casserole. Add the onion and garlic and fry until softened.

Drain the tomatoes thoroughly, then mash to a pulp. Add to the onion, together with the oregano, paprika, basil and wine. Season with salt and pepper to taste. Cook gently for 10 minutes.

Gradually stir in the Cheddar and cook over a low heat until melted. Check and adjust the seasoning if necessary. Serve immediately with the bread cubes. Dip these into the hot fondue before eating.

Serves 4

Fried Apple and Cheese Sandwiches

2 dessert apples, peeled, cored and grated
125 g (4 oz) Cheddar cheese, grated
125 g (4 oz) cream cheese
dash of Tabasco sauce
8 slices wholemeal bread, buttered
50 g (2 oz) butter
salt and pepper

Place the apple, Cheddar, cream cheese and Tabasco in a bowl. Mix until thoroughly blended. Season with salt and pepper to taste.

Divide the mixture between 4 of the bread slices and spread evenly. Cover with the remaining bread.

Melt half the butter in a frying pan. Add 2 of the sandwiches and fry gently on both sides until golden and the cheese is slightly melted. Repeat with the remaining butter and sandwiches. Serve immediately with a crisp green salad, if you like.

Serves 4

right from top: savoury onion puffs; tomato fondue; fried apple and cheese sandwiches

Piperade Baps

1 tablespoons vegetable oil

50 g (2 oz) butter

1 large onion, chopped

1 garlic clove, crushed (optional)

1 green pepper, cored, deseeded and cut into thin strips

4 rashers streaky bacon, rinded and diced

4 eggs, beaten

4½ teaspoons cold water

4 floury baps, warmed

salt and pepper

Heat the oil and 15 g (½ oz) of the butter in a 20–23 cm (8–9 inch) frying pan. Add the onion, garlic, if using, the green pepper and bacon and fry over a low heat for about 15 minutes, stirring from time to time.

Meanwhile, whisk the eggs together with the water and season with salt and pepper to taste. Pour into the onion mixture in the pan and stir lightly with a fork. Cook over a low heat for about 3 minutes, or until the mixture is golden brown on the underside.

Place the pan under a preheated hot grill for 2–3 minutes until the mixture is set on top. Turn on to a board and cut into quarters. Split the baps and spread with the remaining butter. Place an omelette quarter in each bap and serve immediately.

Serves 4

Beef and Onion Patties

½ x 75 g (3 oz) packet instant mashed potato

5 tablespoons milk

5 tablespoons water

200 g (7 oz) corned beef

1 onion, finely chopped

50 g (2 oz) fresh white breadcrumbs

2 teaspoons Worcestershire sauce

2 teaspoons French mustard

2 eggs, beaten

2 tablespoons vegetable oil

salt and pepper

green salad, to serve

Make up the potato as directed on the packet, using the milk and water.

Place the corned beef in a bowl and mash with a fork. Add the onion, potato, breadcrumbs, Worcestershire sauce, mustard and eggs. Beat until thoroughly mixed. Season with salt and pepper to taste.

Heat the oil in a frying pan and add tablespoonfuls of the mixture. Fry gently for about 5 minutes on each side until firm and golden.

Remove and drain thoroughly on kitchen paper.

Serve hot, accompanied by a crisp green or mixed salad.

Serves 4

Ham and Mushroom Toasts

300 ml (½ pint) packet onion sauce mix

300 ml (½ pint) milk

375 g (12 oz) button mushrooms, sliced

125 g (4 oz) cooked ham, diced

125 ml (4 fl oz) natural yogurt

4 slices brown or white bread, toasted and buttered

pepper

sprigs of parsley, to garnish

Put the sauce mix in a pan, stir in the milk and heat gently until thickened.

Add the mushrooms and ham. Cover and simmer for 5 minutes, or until the mushrooms are tender.

Remove from the heat and stir in the yogurt. Spoon over the buttered toast and sprinkle with pepper to taste. Garnish with parsley and serve immediately.

Serves 4

Note: This recipe is equally delicious prepared with tongue instead of ham.

right: beef and onion patties;
far right: ham and mushroom toasts

Baked Cheese and Mustard Pudding

4 thick slices brown or white bread,
  crusts removed
50 g (2 oz) butter
1–2 tablespoons English mustard
175 g (6 oz) Cheddar cheese, grated
2 eggs
2 egg yolks
150 ml (¼ pint) chicken stock
pepper
tomato slices to garnish

Spread both sides of the bread thickly with the butter and mustard to taste.

Thoroughly grease a pie dish with butter. Put 2 slices of bread in the dish, cover with half the Cheddar and sprinkle with a little pepper. Top with the remaining bread.

Beat together the eggs and egg yolks and stir in the stock. Pour over the bread and top with the remaining cheese.

Cook in a preheated oven, 190°C (375°F), Gas Mark 5, for 25–30 minutes until golden.

Garnish with tomato slices and serve immediately.

Serves 4

Baked Eggs in Orange Potatoes

75 g (3 oz) packet instant mashed
  potato
150 ml (¼ pint) milk
150 ml (¼ pint) water
½ small onion, finely chopped
grated rind of 1 orange
2 egg yolks
2 slices cooked ham, finely chopped
4 eggs
50 g (2 oz) Cheddar cheese, grated
25 g (1 oz) butter
salt and pepper
sprigs of watercress, to garnish

Make up the potato as directed on the packet, using the milk and water. Season liberally with salt and pepper and beat in the onion, orange rind and egg yolks.

Spread in a shallow ovenproof dish and make 4 hollows in the potato mixture. Line each hollow with chopped ham and carefully break an egg into each. Sprinkle the eggs with the Cheddar and dot with butter.

Sprinkle with pepper to taste and bake in a preheated oven, 190°C (375°F), Gas Mark 5, for 20 minutes, or until the eggs are firm.

Garnish with sprigs of watercress and serve immediately.

Serves 4

Eggs Mimosa

4 hard-boiled eggs
40 g (1½ oz) can lumpfish roe
6–8 tablespoons mayonnaise
1 small lettuce, to garnish
thinly sliced brown bread, to serve

Halve the eggs lengthways, remove the yolks and arrange the whites in a serving dish. Fill the egg white hollows with the roe.

Rub the yolks through a sieve and spoon over the roe, reserving about 1 tablespoon to garnish.

Spoon the mayonnaise over the eggs, covering them completely.

Garnish with the reserved egg yolk and lettuce. Serve with thin slices of brown bread.

Serves 4

*far left: baked cheese and mustard
pudding;*
left: baked eggs in orange potatoes

Spanish Omelette

1 tablespoon olive oil

1 garlic clove, crushed

2 onions, sliced

125 g (4 oz) sweetcorn kernels

125 g (4 oz) can pimientos, drained
   and sliced

1 potato, boiled and diced

50 g (2 oz) frozen peas

50 g (2 oz) chorizo or garlic sausage,
   chopped

8 eggs

2 tablespoons water

25 g (1 oz) butter

salt and pepper

sprigs of watercress, to garnish

Heat the oil in a frying pan. Add the garlic and onions and fry over a low heat for 5–8 minutes until soft.

Place the sweetcorn, pimientos, potato, peas and sausage in a bowl. Mix together, then add the onion and garlic.

In a large bowl, beat the eggs together with salt and pepper to taste and add the water. Stir in the vegetable mixture.

Melt the butter in a large frying pan. When sizzling, pour in the omelette mixture and cook over a moderate heat for 5 minutes, or until set, drawing the cooked edges towards the centre during the first minute.

Cut the omelette into quarters and turn out on to warm serving plates. Garnish with watercress and serve immediately.

Serves 4

Macaroni Special

500 g (1 lb) macaroni

4 rashers bacon, rinded and chopped

2 onions, chopped

2 x 300 ml (½ pint) packets cheese
  sauce mix

600 ml (1 pint) milk

125 ml (4 fl oz) single cream

175 g (6 oz) Cheddar cheese, grated

400 g (14 oz) can tomatoes, drained
  and chopped

salt

To garnish:

tomato slices

sprigs of parsley

Smoked Haddock Soufflé Omelette

50 g (2 oz) butter

2 smoked haddock fillets, cooked
  and flaked

5 tablespoons single cream

4 tablespoons grated Parmesan
  cheese

6 eggs, separated

salt and pepper

sprigs of parsley, to garnish

---

*above left: smoked haddock soufflé
omelette;*
above right: macaroni special

Melt half the butter in a saucepan. Add the haddock, cream and half the Parmesan and heat gently until the cheese is melted.

Remove from the heat and season with salt and pepper to taste. Stir in the egg yolks. Whisk the egg whites until stiff and fold gently into the haddock mixture.

Melt the remaining butter in a large frying pan. When sizzling, pour in the omelette mixture. Cook gently for 2–3 minutes until set, drawing the cooked edges towards the centre with a fork.

Cut the omelette into quarters and turn out on to warm serving plates. Sprinkle with the remaining cheese and garnish with parsley. Serve immediately.

Serves 4

Cook the macaroni in boiling salted water for 10 minutes, or until tender, but still firm to the bite.

Cook the bacon in a frying pan over a low heat until crisp. Add the onions and fry gently for 5 minutes.

Make up the cheese sauce with the milk as directed on the packet, then add to the pan. Stir in the cream and half the Cheddar. Cook gently until the cheese is melted.

Drain the macaroni and add to the sauce, together with the tomatoes. Mix well, then turn into a shallow flameproof dish and top with the remaining cheese. Place under a preheated hot grill for about 10 minutes, or until the top is crisp and brown. Garnish with tomato and parsley and serve.

Serves 4

Creamed Mushrooms on Toast

50 g (2 oz) butter

1 small onion, finely chopped

juice of 1 lemon

250 g (8 oz) button mushrooms, sliced

4 teaspoons cornflour

350 ml (12 fl oz) single cream

2 teaspoons curry paste

4 slices wholemeal bread, toasted and buttered

salt and pepper

chopped parsley, to garnish

Melt the butter in a frying pan. Add the onion and fry gently until soft but not browned. Add the lemon juice and mushrooms and fry gently for 3 minutes.

Stir in the cornflour and cook, stirring, for 2 minutes. Gradually add the cream and cook gently, without boiling, until thickened. Add the curry paste and season with salt and pepper to taste.

Divide the mixture between the hot toast slices. Garnish with parsley and serve immediately.

Serves 4

Roe-stuffed Baked Tomatoes

40 g (1½ oz) butter

1 small onion, finely chopped

50 g (2 oz) fresh white breadcrumbs

125 g (4 oz) can smoked cod's roe

grated rind of ½ lemon

pinch of cayenne pepper

4 large tomatoes, halved, deseeded and drained

2–3 tablespoons dry white wine

salt and pepper

black olives, to garnish

Melt 25 g (1 oz) of the butter in a frying pan. Add the onion and fry until soft but not browned. Add the breadcrumbs and fry until golden. Reserve 4 teaspoons of the mixture.

Break up the cod's roe and stir it into the larger quantity of breadcrumb mixture, together with the lemon rind and cayenne. Season with salt and pepper to taste.

Fill the tomato halves with the cod's roe mixture. Spoon the wine over the filling. Sprinkle with the reserved breadcrumb mixture and dot with the remaining butter.

Cook in a preheated oven, 180°C (350°F), Gas Mark 4, for 15–20 minutes until the tomatoes are just tender. Serve hot, garnished with olives.

Serves 4

*above left: creamed mushrooms on toast; **above right:** roe-stuffed baked tomatoes*

French Toasts with Bacon

8 rashers lean bacon, derinded
3 large eggs
4 tablespoons milk
4 thick slices brown or white bread
25 g (1 oz) butter or margarine
salt and pepper

Place a frying pan over a low heat, add the bacon and fry gently in its own fat until quite crisp. Remove from the pan with a slotted spoon and keep warm.

Beat the eggs and milk together, with salt and pepper to taste. Place the bread in a shallow dish and pour over the egg mixture. Leave to soak for a few minutes.

Add the butter to the frying pan and melt over a low heat. Add the bread slices, using a fish slice, and fry both sides until golden brown. Transfer to serving plates and arrange the bacon slices on top. Serve immediately.

Serves 4

English Rarebit

50 g (2 oz) butter
300 ml (½ pint) beer
375 g (12 oz) mature Cheddar cheese
4½ teaspoons cornflour
4½ teaspoons Meaux mustard
1 teaspoon anchovy essence
1 teaspoon Worcestershire sauce
4 slices wholemeal bread, toasted
   and buttered
salt and pepper
sprigs of parsley, to garnish

Melt the butter in a pan. Add half the beer and the Cheddar. Heat gently until the cheese is melted.

Blend the cornflour with the remaining beer and add to the pan. Cook gently until the mixture thickens, then add the mustard, anchovy essence, Worcestershire sauce and salt to taste.

Arrange the toast slices in a shallow flameproof dish and pour the cheese mixture over them. Place the dish under a preheated hot grill for about 3–4 minutes until golden and bubbling.

Sprinkle with pepper to taste and garnish with parsley. Serve immediately.

Serves 4

right from top: english rarebit; creamy herbed noodles; egg and onion casserole

Creamy Herbed Noodles

500 g (1 lb) noodles
50 g (2 oz) butter
1 small onion, finely chopped
1 garlic clove, crushed
300 ml (½ pint) single cream
250 ml (8 fl oz) dry white wine
2 tomatoes, skinned, deseeded
   and chopped
1 teaspoon green peppercorns
   (optional)
2 tablespoons chopped chives
4 mint leaves, chopped
salt and pepper
4 tablespoons grated Parmesan
   cheese, to garnish

Cook the noodles in boiling salted water for 9 minutes, or until tender but still firm to the bite.

Meanwhile, melt the butter in a pan. Add the onion and garlic and fry over a low heat until soft and translucent. Add the cream, wine, tomatoes and peppercorns, if using, and heat to just below boiling point. Simmer gently for 4 minutes.

Drain the noodles and place in a warm serving dish. Add the chives and mint to the sauce. Check and adjust the seasoning if necessary, adding pepper if green peppercorns have not been used. Pour over the noodles.

Sprinkle with Parmesan to garnish and serve immediately.

Serves 4

Egg and Onion Casserole

25 g (1 oz) butter
300 ml (½ pint) milk
2 small onions, finely chopped
300 ml (½ pint) packet onion sauce
   mix
4 hard-boiled eggs, roughly chopped
4 tablespoons fresh white
   breadcrumbs

Melt the butter in a pan. Add the milk and onions and bring to the boil over a moderate heat. Lower the heat, cover and simmer gently for 4 minutes.

Cool slightly, then gradually stir into the onion sauce mix. Return to the heat and cook until thickened.

Stir in the egg, pour into a small flameproof casserole dish and cover with the breadcrumbs.

Place under a preheated hot grill for 3 minutes, or until the crumbs are crisp and golden. Serve immediately.

Serves 4

Prawn-stuffed Cucumbers

1 large cucumber, cut into 8 pieces
75 g (3 oz) cream cheese
2 tablespoons lemon juice
125 g (4 oz) cooked peeled prawns
125 g (4 oz) pimientos, drained and
  chopped

8 mint leaves, chopped
paprika
salt and pepper
thinly sliced buttered brown bread,
  to serve

Hollow out the centre of each cucumber section to form cups and stand upright on a serving dish.

Mix the cream cheese and lemon juice together. Set aside 8 prawns to garnish. Add the remainder to the cheese mixture, together with the pimientos and mint. Season with paprika, salt and pepper to taste and mix well.

Pile the filling into the cucumber cups and garnish with the reserved prawns. Serve with thin slices of buttered brown bread.

Serves 4

Eggs Florentine

750 g (1½ lb) frozen leaf spinach, thawed and well drained
50 g (2 oz) butter
grated nutmeg
4 eggs
4 tablespoons grated Parmesan cheese
salt and pepper
wholemeal bread, to serve (optional)

Place the spinach and half the butter in a large pan. Add grated nutmeg and season with salt and pepper to taste. Cook over a low heat for about 2–3 minutes until tender. Transfer to a shallow ovenproof dish.

Make 4 hollows in the spinach and carefully break an egg into each. Sprinkle 1 tablespoon of Parmesan over each egg and dot with the remaining butter.

Cook in a preheated oven, 180°C (350°F), Gas Mark 4, for about 15 minutes, or until the eggs are cooked through.

Sprinkle with pepper. Serve immediately, accompanied by wholemeal bread if you like.

Serves 4

Curried Egg Salad

150 ml (¼ pint) mayonnaise
4 tablespoons double cream
1 tablespoon curry paste
6 hard-boiled eggs, quartered
1 crisp lettuce, leaves separated
salt and pepper
salad cress or watercress, to garnish

Place the mayonnaise, double cream and curry paste in a large bowl and mix thoroughly. Season with salt and pepper to taste and then carefully fold in the eggs.

Line a serving dish with the lettuce leaves. Arrange the egg mixture in the centre and garnish with the salad cress or watercress. Serve immediately.

Serves 4

right: eggs florentine;
far right: curried egg salad

Asparagus Gratinée

4 slices wholemeal bread, toasted
  and buttered
375 g (12 oz) can asparagus spears,
  drained
50 g (2 oz) Cheddar cheese, grated
pepper

Arrange the buttered toast in a
shallow flameproof dish. Divide the
asparagus spears equally between
the toast slices and sprinkle with
the Cheddar.

   Place under a preheated hot grill
for about 4 minutes, until the
cheese has melted and is lightly
browned. Sprinkle with pepper to
taste and serve immediately.

Serves 4

left: asparagus gratinée;
right: salmon savoury

Cod Bites

These tasty and crispy cod strips are easy to prepare and are sure to be popular with the whole family. Serve hot with tartare sauce.

500 g (1 lb) cod fillets, skinned and
   boned
3 tablespoons plain flour
150 g (5 oz) fresh white breadcrumbs
1½ tablespoons grated Parmesan
   cheese
2 tablespoons parsley
2 eggs, beaten
vegetable oil, for frying
salt and pepper
lemon wedges, to garnish

Cut the cod fillets diagonally into 5 cm x 5 mm (2 x ¼ inch) strips, about 1 cm (½ inch) thick.

Season the flour with salt and pepper to taste and spread out on a plate. Combine the breadcrumbs, Parmesan and parsley and spread out on a separate plate. Toss the cod in the flour, dip into the egg, then coat in the breadcrumb mixture.

Heat the oil in a deep-fryer to 180–190°C (350–375°F) or until a cube of bread browns in 30 seconds. Fry half of the cod for 6–7 minutes until lightly golden brown and cooked through. Drain on kitchen paper and keep warm. Cook the remainder in the same way.

Garnish with lemon wedges and serve hot.

Serves 2–3

Salmon Savoury

2 x 250 g (8 oz) cans salmon, drained
   and mashed
250 g (8 oz) Cheddar cheese, grated
4 tablespoons natural low-fat yogurt
4 tablespoons lemon juice
paprika
4 eggs, beaten
4 slices wholemeal bread, toasted
   and buttered
salt and pepper
lemon wedges, to serve

Mix the salmon with the Cheddar. Stir in the yogurt and lemon juice. Season with salt, pepper and paprika to taste. Stir until well mixed, then beat in the eggs.

Put the toast in a shallow flameproof dish and pile the salmon on top. Place under a preheated low grill for 10 minutes, until heated through, then increase the heat and grill for 5 minutes to brown the top. Serve hot with lemon wedges.

Serves 4

Main Courses

Fish Pie

375 g (12 oz) haddock or cod fillet
250 g (8 oz) mushrooms, sliced
250 g (8 oz) can tomatoes
125 g (4 oz) cooked peeled prawns
300 ml (½ pint) packet onion sauce mix
200 ml (7 fl oz) milk
150 ml (¼ pint) white wine
65 g (2½ oz) packet instant mashed
   potato
6–7 tablespoons water
25 g (1 oz) butter
salt and pepper
To garnish:
tomato slices
sprigs of parsley

Cut the fish fillets into large pieces
and place in a casserole. Cover with
the mushrooms and tomatoes and
pour over a little of the tomato
juice. Sprinkle the prawns on top.

Make the onion sauce as directed
on the packet, using 150 ml (¼ pint)
of the milk and the wine. Pour over
the prawns. Make up the potato as
directed on the packet, using the
remaining milk and the water.
Season to taste. Spoon over the fish
mixture. Dot with the butter.

Bake in a preheated oven, 180°C
(350°F) Gas Mark 4, for 20–25
minutes, until the top is golden.
Garnish with tomato and parsley.

Serves 4

Pacific Tuna Pie

butter, for greasing
2 x 200 g (7 oz) cans tuna fish,
   drained and flaked
375 g (12 oz) can sweetcorn kernels,
   drained
125 g (4 oz) frozen peas
300 g (10 oz) can condensed chicken
   soup
400 g (13 oz) can tomatoes, drained
75 g (3 oz) Cheddar cheese, grated
75 g (3 oz) packet potato crisps,
   crushed
baked tomatoes, to serve (optional)

Grease a casserole with butter. Mix
together the tuna, sweetcorn, peas
and soup. Turn into the casserole
and cover with the tomatoes.

Mix together the cheese and
crisps and sprinkle over the
tomatoes. Cook in a preheated
oven, 190°C (375°F), Gas Mark 5,
for 20 minutes, until the top is
golden and bubbling. Serve hot,
with baked tomatoes if you like.

Serves 4

Baked Trout

50 g (2 oz) butter
4 trout, cleaned
1 lemon, sliced
5 tablespoons dry white wine
1 teaspoon dried tarragon
salt and pepper
parsley, to garnish

Line an ovenproof dish with a large
piece of foil, allowing sufficient to
hang over the sides. Spread the
butter over the foil. Lay the trout in
the dish and arrange the lemon
slices on top.

Mix together the wine, tarragon
and salt and pepper to taste and
pour over the fish.

Fold the foil over the trout to
make a parcel and fold the edges
together to seal. Cook in a
preheated oven, 180°C (350°F),
Gas Mark 4, for 25–30 minutes.

Transfer the trout to a warm
serving dish. Pour over the juices
and garnish with parsley.

Serves 4

*right (clockwise from top left): fish
pie; pacific tuna pie; baked trout*

Plaice in Orange Mayonnaise

butter, for greasing
4 plaice, skinned and filleted
grated rind and juice of 2 oranges
juice of 1 lemon
150 ml (¼ pint) mayonnaise
salt and pepper
To garnish:
anchovy fillets
orange segments

Grease an ovenproof dish with butter. Sprinkle the fish with the rind and juice of 1 orange, the lemon juice and salt and pepper to taste. Roll up each fillet and place in the dish. Cover and cook in a preheated oven, 180°C (350°F), Gas Mark 4, for 20 minutes, or until just tender. Leave to cool.

Add the remaining grated orange rind and juice to the mayonnaise and mix well.

Place the fish in a serving dish and pour over the mayonnaise. Garnish with anchovy fillets and orange segments. Serve cold.

Serves 4

Crunchy Salmon Salad

3 tablespoons mayonnaise
6 tablespoons lemon juice
2 x 200 g (7 oz) cans red salmon
2 dessert apples, peeled, cored and diced
175 g (6 oz) salted peanuts, chopped
1 lettuce
salt and pepper

Mix the mayonnaise and lemon juice together in a bowl. Drain the salmon, flake and add to the mayonnaise mixture. Stir in the apples and peanuts and season with salt and pepper to taste.

Line a serving dish with lettuce leaves and pile the salmon mixture into the centre.

Serves 4

Tuna and Bean Salad

3 tablespoons olive oil
1 tablespoon white wine vinegar
½ teaspoon Dijon mustard
½ teaspoon sugar
125 g (4 oz) and 200 g (7 oz) cans tuna fish, drained and flaked
425 g (14 oz) can butter beans, drained
salt and pepper
chopped capers, to garnish

Put the olive oil, vinegar, mustard and sugar in a screw-top jar and season to taste with salt and pepper. Shake vigorously to mix.

Place the tuna and butter beans in a bowl and mix together. Pour the dressing over the mixture and toss well to coat.

Turn into a serving dish and garnish with capers.

Serves 4

left from the top: plaice in orange mayonnaise; crunchy salmon salad; tuna and bean salad

Seafood Curry

2 tablespoons oil

2 onions, chopped

½ red pepper, cored, deseeded and
    chopped

2 celery sticks, chopped

50 g (2 oz) mushrooms, sliced

4½ teaspoons curry powder

½ teaspoon ground turmeric

½ teaspoon ground ginger

1 cooking apple, peeled, cored
    and diced

250 g (8 oz) haddock fillet

125 g (4 oz) cooked peeled prawns

50 g (2 oz) raisins

1 teaspoon Worcestershire sauce

2 teaspoons tomato purée

6 tablespoons white wine

6 tablespoons water

2 tablespoons natural yogurt

juice of ½ lemon

salt and pepper

twist of lemon, to garnish (optional)

boiled rice, to serve

Heat the oil in a large pan. Add the
onions, red pepper, celery and
mushrooms and fry over a low heat
for 5 minutes. Add the curry
powder, turmeric and ginger and
cook, stirring, for 2 minutes.

Add the apple, haddock, prawns,
raisins, Worcestershire sauce and
tomato purée to the mixture and
stir well. Stir in the wine and water
and season with salt and pepper to
taste. Cover the pan and simmer
gently for 10 minutes.

Just before serving, stir in the
yogurt and lemon juice. Serve with
rice and a lemon garnish, if liked.

Serves 4

Cod in Caper Mayonnaise

4 cod fillets, skinned
150 ml (¼ pint) dry white wine
½ lemon, sliced
6 tablespoons mayonnaise
4 tablespoons lemon juice
50 g (2 oz) capers, chopped
salt and pepper

Place the fish in a frying pan and sprinkle with salt and pepper to taste. Add the wine and lemon slices, cover and simmer for 20 minutes.

Remove the fish from the pan, reserving 2 tablespoons of the cooking liquid, and leave to cool.

Mix together the mayonnaise, lemon juice and the reserved cooking liquid. Stir in the capers.

Place the fish in a serving dish, top with the caper sauce and serve.

Serves 4

Baked Fish with Limes

butter, for greasing
4–6 haddock fillets, fresh or frozen
    and defrosted
finely grated rind and juice of 1 lime
15–25 g (½–1 oz) butter, melted
pepper
To garnish:
sprigs of watercress
lime slices
To serve:
boiled rice
green beans, broccoli or peas
grilled tomatoes
wholemeal rolls or French bread

Lightly grease a shallow ovenproof dish with butter. Put the fish fillets into the dish, sprinkle with the lime rind and season with pepper to taste. Pour the lime juice over the fillets and brush a little butter on each fillet.

Bake in a preheated oven, 190°C (375°F), Gas Mark 5, for about 15–20 minutes, depending on the thickness of the fillets.

Garnish each fillet with watercress and lime slices.

Serve with rice, green beans, broccoli or peas, grilled tomatoes and wholemeal rolls or crusty French bread.

Serves 4–6

left: cod in caper mayonnaise

Haddock and Egg Mornay

4 smoked haddock fillets,
  skinned
450 ml (¾ pint) milk
1 bouquet garni
4 eggs
40 g (1½ oz) butter
40 g (1½ oz) plain flour
75 g (3 oz) Cheddar cheese
pepper
sprigs of parsley, to garnish

Place the haddock in a pan with the milk and bouquet garni. Cook over a low heat for 10 minutes, or until tender. Transfer to a warm serving dish, using a slotted spoon, and keep hot. Strain the milk and reserve.

Poach the eggs in simmering water for 4–5 minutes. Meanwhile, gently melt the butter in a pan. Stir in the flour and cook, stirring, for 2 minutes. Blend in the reserved milk and simmer, stirring, until the mixture has thickened. Stir in two-thirds of the Cheddar.

Using a slotted spoon, place a poached egg on each haddock fillet. Top with the cheese sauce and sprinkle with the remaining cheese and pepper to taste. Place under a preheated hot grill until lightly browned. Serve immediately, garnished with parsley.

Serves 4

below: haddock and egg mornay;
right: chicken with oranges and almonds

Chicken with Lemon

1 tablespoon oil
1 onion, finely chopped
1 garlic clove, crushed
2–3 boneless, skinless chicken breasts,
  cut into thin slices
1 tablespoon soy sauce
50 g (2 oz) button mushrooms, sliced
finely grated rind of 1 lemon
4 tablespoons water
2 tablespoons single cream or milk
pepper
sprigs of watercress, to garnish

Heat the oil in a pan. Add the onion and cook, stirring, for 2 minutes. Stir in the garlic and push to one side of the pan. Tilt the pan to let the juices run out over the base.

Add the chicken and stir-fry for 2 minutes over a high heat. Lower the heat, add the soy sauce and mushrooms. Stir-fry for 1 minute. Stir in the lemon rind and water. Add the cream or milk and heat through gently, without boiling. Season with pepper to taste. Garnish with watercress and serve.

Serves 4

Chicken with Oranges and Almonds

50 g (2 oz) butter
50 g (2 oz) flaked almonds
4 chicken portions
paprika
3 oranges
2 teaspoons caster sugar
salt and pepper

Melt the butter in a pan. Add the almonds and fry over a low heat until golden. Remove with a slotted spoon and set aside.

Sprinkle the chicken with salt, pepper and paprika to taste. Add to the pan and fry, turning, until golden all over. Cover and cook over a low heat for 20 minutes, or until tender.

Meanwhile, squeeze the juice from 2 of the oranges. Carefully cut the third orange into segments, discarding all the pith.

Transfer the chicken to a warm serving dish and keep hot.

Add the orange juice, orange segments and sugar to the pan juices and boil rapidly for 2 minutes. Pour over the chicken. Sprinkle with the almonds to garnish and serve immediately with a green vegetable.

Serves 4

Spiced Country Chicken

4 chicken portions
2 tablespoons plain flour
25 g (1 oz) butter
1 onion, finely chopped
1 garlic clove, crushed
1 green pepper, cored, deseeded and
   chopped
2 teaspoons curry powder
1 teaspoon chopped thyme
250 g (8 oz) can tomatoes
2 tablespoons sweet white vermouth
50 g (2 oz) raisins
salt and pepper
jacket potatoes or boiled rice, to serve

Coat the chicken portions with flour. Melt the butter in a large pan. Add the chicken and fry briskly until golden all over. Remove from the pan and set aside.

Add the onion, garlic, green pepper, curry powder and thyme and fry, stirring, for 5 minutes. Add the tomatoes, together with their juice, and the vermouth. Return the chicken to the pan and season with salt and pepper to taste. Cover and cook for 20 minutes, or until the chicken is tender.

Stir in the raisins and serve hot, with jacket potatoes or boiled rice.

Serves 4

Pork Fillet with Plums

2 tablespoons plain flour
500 g (1 lb) pork fillet, cut into
   4 pieces
50 g (2 oz) butter
1 x 500 g (1 lb) can Victoria plums,
   drained and pitted
¼ teaspoon ground cinnamon
150 ml (¼ pint) red wine
salt and pepper
chopped parsley, to garnish

Season the flour with salt and pepper and toss the pork in the seasoned flour to coat well.

Melt the butter gently in a large frying pan. Add the pork and fry until golden brown on both sides. Transfer to a casserole.

Mash the plums to a coarse purée. Stir in the cinnamon and wine and pour over the pork. Cover and cook in a preheated oven, 180°C (350°F), Gas Mark 4, for 20 minutes.

Serve hot, garnished with parsley.

Serves 4

Pork Chops with Mustard Sauce

25 g (1 oz) butter
1 onion, finely chopped
1 tablespoon flour
4 pork chops
125 ml (4 fl oz) medium sherry
175 ml (6 fl oz) chicken stock
2 tablespoons light French mustard
salt and pepper

Melt the butter in a flameproof casserole. Add the onion and fry until soft. Remove with a slotted spoon and set aside.

Season the flour with salt and pepper and toss the chops in the flour to coat well. Add the chops to the casserole and fry briskly until browned on both sides.

Return the onion to the casserole and add the sherry and stock. Cover and simmer for 20 minutes, or until the chops are cooked.

Transfer the chops to a warm serving dish, using a slotted spoon. Add the mustard to the sauce in the casserole, stir well and check and adjust the seasoning if necessary. Pour the mustard sauce over the chops and serve immediately.

Serves 4

left: pork fillet with plums;
below: pork chops with mustard sauce

Tyrolean Veal with Soured Cream

2 tablespoons plain flour
4 veal escalopes
50 g (2 oz) butter
1 small onion, finely chopped
2 tablespoons capers, with their
   vinegar
200 ml (7 fl oz) water
5 tablespoons soured cream
salt and pepper
chopped parsley, to garnish
boiled rice, to serve

Season half the flour with salt and pepper and use to coat the escalopes.

Melt half the butter in a frying pan. Add the veal and fry gently for about 5 minutes on each side until tender and golden. Remove and set aside.

Melt the remaining butter in the pan. Add the onion and fry until soft. Add the remaining flour and cook, stirring, for 1–2 minutes.

Add the capers in their vinegar and the water and cook until the sauce thickens. Stir in the soured cream. Return the veal to the pan and heat through gently.

Sprinkle with parsley and serve hot with boiled rice.

Serves 4

Turkey Breast with Ham and Cheese

plain flour, for coating
500 g (1 lb) boned turkey breast, cut
   into 4 x 5 mm (¼ inch) thick slices
1 egg, beaten
2 tablespoons vegetable oil
25 g (1 oz) butter
4 slices cooked ham
150 g (5 oz) bel paese or mozzarella
   cheese, thinly sliced
salt and pepper
sprigs of parsley, to garnish
green beans or courgettes, to serve
   (optional)

Season the flour with salt and pepper. Dip the turkey slices into the egg and then into the seasoned flour. Heat the oil and butter in a large frying pan. Add the turkey and fry for about 4 minutes on each side. Drain the turkey slices and transfer them to a grill rack.

Cover each portion of turkey with a slice of ham, then with a slice of cheese. Place under a preheated hot grill and cook for 1 minute, until the cheese is golden and bubbling. Garnish with parsley and serve immediately, with green beans or courgettes, if you like.

Serves 4

Veal Strogonoff

4 veal escalopes

50 g (2 oz) butter

1 onion, sliced

125 g (4 oz) button mushrooms,
  sliced

1–2 tablespoons tomato purée

1 tablespoon plain flour

150 ml (¼ pint) soured cream

1–2 tablespoons lemon juice

salt and pepper

sprigs of watercress, to garnish

buttered noodles or boiled rice,
  to serve

Beat the escalopes with a meat mallet or rolling pin until thin, then cut into short strips.

Melt half the butter in a frying pan. Add the onion and mushrooms and fry until soft. Stir in the tomato purée and flour. Cook, stirring, over a low heat for 2–3 minutes. Remove from the heat.

Melt the remaining butter in a clean pan. Add the veal and fry over a high heat, turning, until evenly browned. Add the meat to the sauce and stir well. Add the soured cream and lemon juice and season with salt and pepper to taste.

Garnish each dish with a sprig of watercress. Serve immediately, with buttered noodles or boiled rice.

Serves 4

left: tyrolean veal with soured cream;
right: veal strogonoff

Tasty Beef Pittas

15 g (½ oz) butter

1½ teaspoons vegetable oil

1 large onion, thinly sliced

375 g (12 oz) minute steak or quick-frying steak, cut into narrow 2.5–5 cm (1–2 inch) strips about 5 mm (¼ inch) thick

4 pitta breads, warmed

3 crisp lettuce leaves, finely shredded

2 tomatoes, chopped

7.5 cm (3 inch) piece cucumber, cut into thin strips

2 tablespoons mayonnaise (optional)

salt and pepper

Heat the butter and oil in a frying pan. Add the onion and cook over a low heat for 3–5 minutes. Add the steak strips and fry over a moderately high heat, stirring frequently, for 5–8 minutes until cooked.

Cut off a small slice from 1 long side of each warmed pitta bread and open out to form a pocket.

Fill the pitta bread two-thirds full with shredded lettuce, tomato and cucumber strips. Top with the fried steak and onions and season with salt and pepper to taste. Add a spoonful of mayonnaise, if using, to each pitta. Serve hot.

Serves 4

right: chilli con carne

Chilli Con Carne

To add a bit more colour to this classic winter warmer, add a roughly chopped green pepper at the same time as the kidney beans.

50 g (2 oz) butter

2 large onions, finely chopped

2 garlic cloves, crushed

500 g (1 lb) minced beef

2 teaspoons chilli powder

4 teaspoons ground cumin

55 g (2¼ oz) can tomato purée

2 x 425 g (14 oz) cans red kidney beans, drained

300 ml (½ pint) beef stock

salt and pepper

chopped parsley or coriander, to garnish

boiled rice or French bread, to serve

Melt the butter in a flameproof casserole. Add the onions and garlic and fry gently for 5 minutes until golden. Stir in the beef and cook, stirring, for 10 minutes.

Mix together the chilli powder, cumin and tomato purée and stir into the beef. Add the kidney beans, stock and salt and pepper to taste.

Cover and cook in a preheated oven, 190°C (375°F), Gas Mark 5, for 15 minutes.

Sprinkle with chopped parsley or coriander and serve hot, with plain boiled rice or crusty French bread.

Serves 4

Beef and Orange Kebabs

500 g (1 lb) frying steak, cut into bite-sized pieces

2–3 tomatoes, quartered

½ green pepper, cored, deseeded and cut into pieces

½ red pepper, cored, deseeded and cut into pieces

125 g (4 oz) button mushrooms

1 onion, cut into segments

2 tablespoons vegetable oil

grated rind and juice of 1 orange

1 tablespoon soft brown sugar

1 tablespoon soy sauce

pepper

sprigs of watercress, to garnish

To serve:

French bread

green salad

Thread the meat and vegetables alternately on 4–6 long skewers or 8–12 smaller ones, starting with the tomatoes.

Mix together the oil, orange rind and juice, sugar and soy sauce and season with pepper to taste. Brush the mixture all over the kebabs.

Cook under a preheated moderate grill for about 15 minutes. Brush the kebabs with the oil and orange mixture after 10 minutes, turn them over and cook for a further 5 minutes. Garnish with watercress.

Serve with crusty French bread and a green salad.

Serves 4–6

Frankfurters, Garlic Sausage and Beans

This hearty dish brings satisfaction with minimal effort. Frankfurters are lightly smoked sausages which are usually packaged precooked so can be reheated quite quickly and easily. They are available in a variety of sizes.

25 g (1 oz) butter
1 large onion, chopped
2 bacon rashers, rinded and chopped
4 frankfurters, diced
125 g (4 oz) garlic sausage, diced
1 tablespoon capers, chopped
2 x 425 g (14 oz) cans red kidney
  beans, drained
150 ml (¼ pint) chicken or beef stock
2 tablespoons chopped parsley
salt and pepper
French bread or boiled white rice, to
  serve

Melt the butter gently in a large flameproof casserole. Add the onion and bacon and fry over a low heat until the onion is softened and the bacon is crisp. Add the frankfurters, garlic sausage, capers and all the kidney beans. Mix thoroughly.

Stir in the stock. Cover the casserole and cook in a preheated oven, 180°C (350°F), Gas Mark 4, for 20 minutes.

Check and adjust the seasoning if necessary and stir in the parsley.

Serve immediately in bowls, accompanied by crusty French bread or served on a bed of boiled white rice.

Serves 4

Roast Beef Salad with Soured Cream and Olives

500 g (1 lb) rare roast beef, thickly
   sliced
175 ml (6 fl oz) soured cream
juice of 1 lemon
125 g (4 oz) black olives, halved
   and pitted
To serve:
jacket potatoes
side salads

Cut the beef slices into strips and
place in a serving dish. Mix together
the soured cream and lemon juice.
Add half the olives to the beef slices
and spoon the soured cream
mixture over the top.

   Garnish with the remaining
olives. Serve with jacket potatoes
and side salads of your choice.

Serves 4

Saucy Liver and Mushroom Pasta

300 ml (½ pint) milk
375 g (12 oz) lamb's liver, cut into
  thin 5 mm x 5 cm (¼ x 2 inch) strips
50 g (2 oz) plain flour
50 g (2 oz) butter
4½ teaspoons vegetable oil
2 large onions, halved and thinly
  sliced
125 g (4 oz) button mushrooms,
  thinly sliced
150 ml (¼ pint) hot chicken stock
4½ teaspoons tomato purée
250 g (8 oz) dried tagliatelle
4½ teaspoons chopped parsley
salt and pepper
To garnish:
sprig of chervil

Put the milk and the strips of liver
in a shallow dish. Turn the liver to
soak in the milk, then remove,
reserving the milk. Spread the flour
out on a plate, season with salt and
pepper and turn the liver in the
seasoned flour to coat thoroughly.

Heat 15 g (½ oz) of the butter and
1½ teaspoons of the oil in a frying
pan. Add the liver strips and fry
over a moderate heat, stirring
frequently, for 3 minutes. Remove
from the pan with a slotted spoon
and set aside on a plate.

Add 25 g (1 oz) of the butter and
the remaining oil to the pan. Add
the onions and mushrooms and fry,
stirring thoroughly, over a low heat
for 3 minutes.

Stir in the stock, reserved milk
and tomato purée and bring to the
boil, stirring. Lower the heat, add
the liver, cover the pan and cook
over a low heat, stirring frequently,
for 12 minutes. Taste and adjust the
seasoning.

Meanwhile, cook the tagliatelle in
a saucepan of boiling, salted water
for 10–12 minutes until tender.

Drain well, rinse with boiling water
and drain well again. Melt the
remaining butter in the rinsed-out
pan and stir in the parsley. Add the
tagliatelle and toss to coat
thoroughly in melted butter.

Spoon the tagliatelle on to a
warm serving dish and spoon the
liver mixture into the centre.
Garnish with chervil and serve.

Serves 4

Liver and Bacon with Apple Rings

50 g (2 oz) butter
2 large cooking apples, peeled, cored
  and cut into thick rings
500 g (1 lb) calf's liver, sliced
4 rashers lean bacon, rinded

Melt half the butter in a frying pan.
Add the apple rings and fry gently
until soft. Transfer to a warm dish
and keep hot.

Gently melt the remaining butter
in the pan. Add the liver and fry
gently for about 2 minutes on each
side until tender.

Meanwhile, cook the bacon under
a preheated moderate grill until
crisp and cooked.

Alternate the liver with the apple
rings on a warmed serving dish.
Arrange the bacon around the edge.
Serve immediately.

Serves 4

Barbecued Lamb Cutlets

8 lamb cutlets, trimmed
boiled rice or buttered noodles,
  to serve
Marinade:
dash of Tabasco sauce
2 teaspoons chilli powder
2 teaspoons salt
4½ teaspoons soft brown sugar
4½ teaspoons Worcestershire sauce
2 tablespoons tomato ketchup
4½ teaspoons wine vinegar
4 tablespoons water

Mix the Tabasco, chilli powder, salt
and brown sugar together in a large
dish. Gradually stir in the
Worcestershire sauce, tomato
ketchup, vinegar and water. Add the
cutlets and turn to coat thoroughly.
Leave to marinate for 10 minutes.

  Transfer the cutlets to a grill rack
and brush thickly with the
marinade. Cook under a preheated
hot grill for 5–10 minutes on each
side, depending on the thickness of
the cutlets, basting frequently with
the marinade.

  Serve immediately with plain
boiled rice or buttered noodles.

Serves 4

left: liver and bacon with apple rings;
right: barbecued lamb cutlets

Vegetarian

Vegetable and Pasta Stir-fry

500 g (1 lb) dried wholewheat
   pasta shells
75 g (3 oz) butter
1 large onion, sliced
3 celery sticks, cut into strips
2 large carrots, cut into strips
75 g (3 oz) French beans
1 small red pepper, cored, deseeded
   and sliced
1 small green or yellow pepper,
   cored, deseeded and sliced
2 tablespoons soy sauce
salt and pepper

Cook the pasta in a pan of boiling
salted water for 8–10 minutes until
tender, but still firm to the bite.
Drain and refresh under cold water.

Melt the butter in a frying pan or
wok. Add the onion, celery, carrots,
beans and peppers. Stir-fry over a
low heat for about 10 minutes.

Add the pasta and soy sauce and
season, blending well. Cook for a
further 2 minutes to reheat the
pasta. Serve hot.

Serves 4

top right: vegetable and pasta
stir-fry;
bottom right: vegetable pilaff

Vegetable Pilaff

50 g (2 oz) butter
1 onion, sliced
1 garlic clove, crushed
2 celery sticks, sliced
250 g (8 oz) brown rice
125 g (4 oz) button mushrooms,
   sliced
325 g (11 oz) can sweetcorn kernels
   with peppers, drained
600 ml (1 pint) vegetable stock
50 g (2 oz) raisins
50 g (2 oz) chopped nuts

Melt the butter in a pan. Add the
onion, garlic and celery and cook
for about 5 minutes until softened.
Add the rice, blending well, and
cook, stirring occasionally, for a
further 5 minutes.

Stir in the mushrooms, sweetcorn
kernels with peppers and stock.
Bring to the boil, then transfer to a
flameproof casserole.

Cover and cook in a preheated
oven, 190°C (375°F), Gas Mark 5,
for 20–25 minutes.

Stir in the raisins and nuts. Add a
little extra stock if necessary. Cover
and cook for a further 5 minutes.
Serve immediately.

Serves 4

Vegetable Curry

2 tablespoons vegetable oil
1 onion, chopped
1 tablespoon curry powder
1 teaspoon paprika
2 teaspoons tomato purée
1 teaspoon lemon juice
1 tablespoon apricot jam
300 ml (½ pint) milk
50 g (2 oz) sultanas
1 kg (2 lb) mixed prepared vegetables
   (e.g. sliced carrots, cauliflower
   florets and diced potato)
4 hard-boiled eggs, sliced or halved
chutney, to serve

Heat the oil in a pan. Add the onion
and fry gently for 5 minutes. Stir in
the curry powder and paprika and
cook for a further 3 minutes.

Add the tomato purée, lemon
juice, jam, milk and sultanas,
blending well. Bring to the boil,
reduce the heat and simmer,
uncovered for 10 minutes.

Meanwhile, cook the vegetables
in a pan of boiling salted water for
10 minutes. Drain well and add to
the curry sauce. Cook over a low
heat for 10 minutes or until the
vegetables are tender.

Add the eggs, mixing well. Spoon
into a warmed serving dish and
serve with a chutney.

Serves 4

Three Bean Curry

125 g (4 oz) butter
2 onions, finely chopped
3 garlic cloves, crushed
1 tablespoon ground coriander
1 teaspoon garam masala
1 teaspoon chilli powder
400 g (13 oz) can chopped tomatoes
1 teaspoon sugar
425 g (14 oz) can butter beans,
   drained
425 g (14 oz) can kidney beans,
   drained
425 g (14 oz) can haricot beans or
   cannellini beans, drained
salt
5–6 sprigs of coriander leaves,
   chopped, to garnish

Melt the butter in a pan. Add the
onions and fry until lightly
browned. Add the garlic and fry for
a few seconds, then add the ground
coriander, garam masala and chilli
powder and stir-fry for a few
seconds. Stir in the tomatoes, with
their juice, season with salt to taste
and add the sugar. Reduce the heat
and simmer for 10 minutes.

Add the beans, stir well, then
cover and heat gently. Garnish with
coriander and serve immediately.

Serves 4

left: okra curry;
right: *potato and eggs bombay*

Okra Curry

250 g (8 oz) okra
2 tablespoons vegetable oil
1 x 2.5 cm (1 inch) piece fresh root
   ginger, chopped
1 teaspoon ground turmeric
300 ml (½ pint) natural yogurt
½ teaspoon chilli powder
2 tablespoons grated fresh coconut
1 tablespoon finely chopped
   coriander leaves
salt

Cut the tops off the okra and halve
lengthways. Heat the oil in a pan.
Add the okra and fry for 5 minutes.
Add the ginger and turmeric, season
with salt to taste and stir well. Add
2–3 tablespoons of water, cover and
cook for 10 minutes until the okra
is tender.

Mix all the remaining ingredients
together, blending well. Add to the
pan and stir thoroughly. Transfer to
a warmed serving dish. Serve hot.

Serves 4

Potato and Eggs Bombay

3 tablespoons olive oil

1 teaspoon cumin seeds

2 teaspoons mustard seeds

750 g (1½ lb) potatoes, scrubbed and
cut into 1 cm (½ inch) cubes

1 teaspoon ground coriander

1 teaspoon garam masala

½ teaspoon ground turmeric

4 eggs

salt and pepper

1 tablespoon chopped coriander, plus
1 sprig of coriander, to garnish

Heat the oil in a heavy-based frying
pan. Add the cumin and mustard
seeds and cook for a few seconds
until the seeds begin to pop.

Stir in the diced potato, ground
coriander, garam masala and
turmeric, blending well. Cover,
reduce the heat and simmer gently
for 15–20 minutes until the potato
is just tender.

Make 4 hollows, evenly spaced,
in the cooked potato mixture and
crack an egg into each hole. Cover
and continue cooking for a further
5 minutes, or until the eggs are set.

Remove from the heat, season
with salt and pepper to taste and
stir in the chopped coriander. Serve
at once, straight from the pan,
garnished with a sprig of coriander.

Serves 4

Two Cheese Spaghetti

500 g (1 lb) dried wholewheat or
   plain spaghetti
65 g (2½ oz) butter
125 g (4 oz) button mushrooms,
   sliced
40 g (1½ oz) flour
600 ml (1 pint) milk
125 g (4 oz) vegetarian Edam cheese,
   grated
75 g (3 oz) vegetarian Cheddar
   cheese, grated
salt and pepper

Cook the pasta in a pan of boiling
salted water for 8–10 minutes until
tender, but still firm to the bite.

Meanwhile, melt 25 g (1 oz) of
the butter in a pan. Add the
mushrooms and sauté for 5 minutes.
Remove from the pan and set aside.

Add the remaining butter to the
pan juices and heat to melt. Stir in
the flour and cook for 1 minute.
Remove from the heat and add the
milk, blending well. Bring to the
boil and cook, stirring constantly,
for 2–3 minutes until smooth.

Add the Edam to the sauce and
season with salt and pepper to taste.

Drain the pasta, return to the pan
and add the mushrooms and cheese
sauce. Mix well, then spoon into a
flameproof dish. Sprinkle with the
Cheddar and cook under a
preheated hot grill until golden.

Serves 4

Pasta with Mushroom and Tomato Sauce

4 teaspoons vegetable oil

1 onion, chopped

1 garlic clove, crushed

400 g (13 oz) can chopped tomatoes
  or 500 g (1 lb) ripe tomatoes,
  skinned, deseeded and chopped

150 g (5 oz) can tomato purée

4 tablespoons red wine or vegetable
  stock

1 tablespoon brown sugar

½ teaspoon dried oregano

½ teaspoon dried basil

175 g (6 oz) cooked sliced
  mushrooms

500 g (1 lb) pasta (e.g. plain or
  spinach tagliatelle or spaghetti)

salt and pepper

Heat the oil in a pan. Add the onion and garlic and cook gently for about 6–8 minutes until just softened but not browned.

Add the tomatoes, tomato purée, wine or stock, sugar, oregano and basil and season with salt and pepper to taste, blending well. Cook the sauce over a low heat for about 20 minutes until thick and pulpy. Stir in the mushrooms and heat them through gently.

Meanwhile, cook the pasta in a large saucepan of boiling salted water for about 8–10 minutes or according to packet instructions until tender, but still firm to the bite.

Serve the sauce hot over the pasta accompanied with warm garlic bread and a mixed green salad.

Serves 4

Crusty Mushroom Loaf

1 small wholemeal crusty loaf
50 g (2 oz) butter
50 g (2 oz) flour
600 ml (1 pint) milk
250 g (8 oz) open cup mushrooms, sliced
2 tablespoons chopped parsley
2 hard-boiled eggs, chopped
salt and pepper
seasonal salad, to serve

Cut a 1 cm (½ inch) slice lengthways off the top of the loaf and carefully pull out the soft bread inside (use to make breadcrumbs for another dish). Replace the lid and place on a baking tray. Cook in a preheated oven, 180°C (350°F), Gas Mark 4, for 15 minutes until crisp.

Meanwhile, to make the filling, melt the butter in a pan. Stir in the flour and cook for 1 minute. Remove from the heat and gradually add the milk, blending well. Bring to the boil and cook, stirring constantly, for 2–3 minutes until smooth and thickened.

Stir in the mushrooms, parsley and eggs and season with salt and pepper to taste, blending well.

Fill the bread loaf shell with the mushroom mixture and replace the lid. Return to the oven and bake for 10 minutes. Serve hot, cut into thick slices with a seasonal salad.

Serves 4

Savoury Tomato and Cheddar Bake

This delicious bake is quick to prepare and can be left to cook on its' own.

6 small field mushrooms, peeled
25 g (1 oz) butter
175 g (6 oz) fresh breadcrumbs
125 g (4 oz) vegetarian Cheddar cheese, grated
½ green pepper, cored, deseeded and chopped
1 onion, finely chopped
50 g (2 oz) walnuts, chopped
1 teaspoon mustard powder
1 teaspoon salt
2 eggs, beaten
3 tomatoes, skinned and sliced
4 tablespoons tomato ketchup
tomato wedges, to garnish

Cut the stalks off the mushrooms and arrange the caps, stalk-side down, along the base of a greased 1 kg (2 lb) loaf tin. Dot the mushrooms with half of the butter.

Mix the breadcrumbs with the Cheddar, green pepper, onion, walnuts, mustard and salt. Stir in the eggs, blending well.

Spoon half of the breadcrumb mixture on top of the mushrooms and press down. Arrange the tomato slices on top and dot with the remaining butter. Stir the tomato ketchup into the remaining breadcrumb mixture. Spoon on top of the tomatoes and press firmly.

Bake in a preheated oven, 200°C (400°F), Gas Mark 6, for 45 minutes. Turn out of the tin onto a warmed serving plate. Garnish with the tomatoes and serve hot with green vegetables or cold with a salad.

Serves 4–6

Cheesy Crust Toasties

crusts cut from a large wholewheat tin loaf
50 g (2 oz) butter
175 g (6 oz) vegetarian Cheddar cheese, grated
5 tomatoes
325 g (11 oz) can sweetcorn kernels, drained

Spread the loaf crusts (4 long pieces and 2 ends of the loaf) with the butter and sprinkle with half the Cheddar. Coarsely chop 2 tomatoes and thinly slice the remainder.

Top the crusts with the sweetcorn and chopped tomatoes. Cover with the remaining cheese and the slices of tomato.

Cook under a preheated moderate grill for 8–10 minutes until the filling is hot and golden. Serve hot.

Serves 4–6

left: crusty mushroom loaf

Curried Cheese Tart

To save time when making this cheese tart, use a pre-cooked flan case instead of making one at the time. This will reduce the cooking time to about 15–20 minutes.

250 g (8 oz) shortcrust pastry, defrosted, if frozen
Filling:
1 tablespoon vegetable oil
1 red pepper, cored, deseeded and sliced
2 tablespoons mango chutney
150 g (5 oz) vegetarian Red Leicester cheese, grated
50 g (2 oz) walnuts, chopped
½–1 teaspoon curry powder
2 eggs, beaten
150 ml (¼ pint) single cream
2 tablespoons chopped parsley
salt and pepper

Roll out the pastry on a lightly floured surface and use to line an 18 cm (7 inch) square flan dish or shallow cake tin. Chill while preparing the filling.

Heat the oil in a pan. Add the red pepper and cook for 5 minutes until softened. Spread the mango chutney over the pastry base and sprinkle with the cooked pepper.

Mix the cheese with the walnuts, curry powder, eggs, cream, parsley and salt and pepper to taste. Pour into the pastry case.

Bake in a preheated oven, 180°C (350°F), Gas Mark 4, for 35–40 minutes. Serve warm or cold.

Serves 6

Spinach and Brie Flan

To save time, use a pre-cooked flan case and reduce the cooking time.

250 g (8 oz) shortcrust pastry, defrosted, if frozen
Filling:
300 g (10 oz) Brie cheese, derinded
125 g (4 oz) spinach leaves, washed and finely shredded
2 eggs
150 ml (¼ pint) milk
3 tablespoons double cream
a pinch of grated nutmeg
salt and pepper

Grease a 20 cm (8 inch) flan ring set on a baking tray and chill.

Roll out the pastry on a lightly floured surface to a round large enough to line the flan ring.

Cut the Brie into cubes. Place the spinach on the pastry base and tuck in the pieces of Brie.

Beat the eggs with the milk and salt and pepper to taste. Pour over the flan. Spoon the cream over the surface and sprinkle with nutmeg.

Bake in a preheated oven, 190°C (375°F), Gas Mark 5, for 35–40 minutes. Serve warm or cold.

Serves 4

Potato and Cheese Pie

750 g (1½ lb) boiled potatoes,
  mashed
grated nutmeg
50 g (2 oz) butter
75 g (3 oz) Cheddar cheese, grated
salt and pepper

To garnish:
tomato slices
sprigs of parsley

Season the potato with salt, pepper and nutmeg to taste and beat in half of the butter. Spread the potato mixture in a shallow ovenproof dish. Top with the Cheddar and the remaining butter.

Cook in a preheated oven, 180°C (350°F), Gas Mark 4, for 15 minutes, then place under a preheated hot grill for 3 minutes.

Sprinkle with pepper and garnish with tomato and parsley. Serve hot.

Serves 4

top left: spinach and brie flan;
bottom left: curried cheese tart;
below: potato and cheese pie

Vegetable and Bean Biryani

4 tablespoons vegetable oil or ghee

¾ teaspoon poppy seeds

1 teaspoon mustard seeds

pinch of cayenne pepper

¼ teaspoon ground turmeric

¾ teaspoon garam masala

¼ teaspoon ground coriander

1 aubergine, cubed

1 red pepper, cored, deseeded
   and sliced

75 g (3 oz) cooked butter beans

2 tomatoes, skinned, deseeded
   and chopped

250 g (8 oz) long-grain brown rice,
   cooked with a little saffron

salt and pepper

To garnish:

toasted pine nuts

raisins

sprigs of coriander

Heat the oil or ghee in a large pan.
Add the poppy and mustard seeds
and cook, stirring, for 2 minutes.

Add the cayenne, turmeric, garam
masala, coriander, aubergine, red
pepper, butter beans and tomatoes
and season to taste. Cover and cook
for about 10 minutes.

Layer the rice and the vegetable
mixture in an ovenproof dish.
Cover and cook in a preheated
oven, 190°C (375°F), Gas Mark 5,
for 20 minutes. Garnish with pine
nuts, raisins and coriander.

Serves 4

Spinach Risotto

500 g (1 lb) spinach, washed

2 tablespoons olive oil

125 g (4 oz) butter

1 small onion, finely chopped

500 g (1 lb) short-grain Italian rice

1.6 litres (2¾ pints) vegetable stock

1 teaspoon dried oregano

1 garlic clove, crushed

75 g (3 oz) Parmesan cheese, grated

salt and pepper

Cook the spinach in a saucepan
without added water, stirring
occasionally, for about 5 minutes
until tender. Drain the spinach very
thoroughly and chop finely.

Heat the oil and half the butter in
a saucepan. Add the onion and fry
for 3 minutes. Add the rice, and stir
over a low heat for 5 minutes,
making sure that the rice is coated
but does not colour.

Add a cupful of the stock and
cook until it has been absorbed.
Add another cup of the stock, the
chopped spinach, oregano and
garlic. Cook until all the stock has
been absorbed. Continue adding
the stock in the same way until it
has all been absorbed and the rice is
tender (about 15 minutes).

Season with salt and pepper to
taste and stir in the remaining
butter and all but 1 tablespoon of
the Parmesan. Pile on to a warm
serving dish and sprinkle with the
remaining cheese. Serve at once.

Serves 4–6

Aubergine and Tomato Bake

To save time, drain the aubergines in advance, so they are ready when preparing the dish.

2 aubergines, cubed
1 onion, chopped
2 garlic cloves, crushed
1–2 tablespoons oil
2 courgettes, diced
400 g (14 oz) can plum tomatoes
1 teaspoon ground cumin
salt and pepper

Topping:
50 g (2 oz) butter or margarine
125 g (4 oz) plain flour
25 g (1 oz) sesame seeds
salt and pepper
knobs of butter

Place the aubergine in a colander, sprinkle with salt and leave to drain for 30 minutes. Rinse, drain and pat dry. Fry the onion and garlic in the oil until soft. Add the aubergine and courgette and fry for a further 5 minutes. Pour in the tomatoes, add the cumin and salt and pepper and bring to the boil.

Rub the fat into the flour until the mixture resembles fine breadcrumbs. Stir in the sesame seeds and salt and pepper. Pour the vegetable mixture into an ovenproof dish, spread the crumble mixture on top and dot with the butter. Bake in a preheated oven 200°C (400°F), Gas Mark 6, for 25–30 minutes, or until the top is golden.

Serves 4

left: spinach risotto
below: *aubergine and tomato bake*

Onion Tortilla

40 g (1½ oz) butter

1 large onion, halved and thinly sliced

125 g (4 oz) cabbage, finely shredded

3 eggs, beaten

1 tablespoon cold water

125 g (4 oz) vegetarian Cheddar or
   Edam cheese, finely grated

salt and pepper

tomato wedges, to garnish

green salad, to serve

Melt 25 g (1 oz) of the butter in a
saucepan. Add the onion and
cabbage and cook over a low heat,
stirring frequently, for 3 minutes.

Beat the eggs with the water and
season with salt and pepper to taste.
Stir in half the cheese.

Melt the remaining butter in a
23 cm (9 inch) frying pan. Add the
onion and cabbage mixture, pour
over the egg and cheese mixture
and cook over a moderately high
heat for 3 minutes, or until lightly
golden on the underside.

Sprinkle the surface of the tortilla
with the remaining cheese and place
under a preheated medium hot grill
for 2–3 minutes until the cheese is
melted and the tortilla is set. Cut
into wedges, garnish with tomatoes
and serve hot with a green salad.

Serves 4

French Bread Pizzas

Vary the topping ingredients according
to personal taste. Pine nuts, olives and
sun-dried tomatoes would make tasty
toppings as well.

1 French loaf, halved lengthways

Base:

65 g (2½ oz) can tomato purée

1–2 teaspoons dried mixed herbs

1–2 cloves garlic, crushed

Topping:

4 tomatoes, sliced

2 tablespoons capers

a few basil leaves

125 g (4 oz) vegetarian Gruyère or
   mozzarella cheese, grated

Spread the cut surfaces of the bread
with the tomato purée. Sprinkle
with the herbs and the garlic.

Arrange the sliced tomatoes on
each piece of French bread. Sprinkle
with the capers and basil and top
with the cheese.

Carefully cut each piece of bread
into 4 slices. Place the pizzas on
lightly oiled baking trays and bake
in a preheated oven, 200°C (400°F),
Gas Mark 6, for 15 minutes. Serve
hot or warm.

Serves 2

top: onion tortilla;
right: crispy corn bake

Crispy Corn Bake

25 g (1 oz) plain flour

2 eggs, beaten

25 g (1 oz) soft brown sugar

25 g (1 oz) butter or margarine, melted

6 tablespoons milk

2 x 325 g (11 oz) cans sweetcorn kernels, drained

75 g (3 oz) potato crisps, crushed

salt and pepper

sprigs of parsley, to garnish

Put the flour in a large bowl and gradually add the eggs, sugar, butter or margarine and milk, beating constantly to create a smooth mixture. Season with salt and pepper to taste and stir in the sweetcorn kernels.

Spoon the mixture into an ovenproof dish and sprinkle the crisps over the top.

Bake in a preheated oven, 190°C (375°F), Gas Mark 5, for 30–35 minutes until golden and firm. Serve hot, garnished with parsley.

Serves 4

Vegetables and Salads

Green and White Vegetable Salad

2 tablespoons olive oil

1 tablespoon walnut oil

1 tablespoon white wine vinegar

½ teaspoon Dijon mustard

½ teaspoon sugar

50 g (2 oz) frozen green peas, thawed

125 g (4 oz) white cabbage, thinly sliced

2 celery sticks, chopped

1 small green pepper, cored, deseeded and chopped

½ onion or ½ leek, thinly sliced

125 g (4 oz) Brussels sprouts, quartered

125 g (4 oz) bean sprouts

Put the olive oil, walnut oil, vinegar, mustard and sugar in a screw-top jar and shake vigorously to mix.

Mix all the vegetables together in a salad bowl. Pour over the dressing and toss well. Serve immediately.

Serves 4

Cabbage Salad with Peanut Dressing

1 small white cabbage, finely sliced

125 g (4 oz) salted peanuts, chopped

2 red peppers, cored, deseeded and finely chopped

1 teaspoon anchovy essence

1 tablespoon soy sauce

2 tablespoons lemon juice

1 teaspoon cayenne pepper

½ teaspoon salt

1 teaspoon soft brown sugar

Put the cabbage in a salad bowl. Combine the remaining ingredients to form a crunchy dressing. Add to the cabbage, toss well and serve immediately.

Serves 4

Vegetable and Nut Salad

250–300 g (8–10 oz) bean sprouts

125–150 g (4–5 oz) cabbage, shredded

1 green chilli, deseeded and very finely chopped

15–20 g (½–¾ oz) fresh ginger root, finely chopped

2–3 sprigs of coriander, chopped

½ cucumber, grated

lemon juice

1 eating apple or 1 ripe fresh mango

50 g (2 oz) unsalted peanuts, roughly chopped

50 g (2 oz) unsalted cashew nuts, roughly chopped

½ coconut, flesh removed and grated

salt

In a large bowl mix together the bean sprouts, cabbage, chilli, ginger and coriander. Discard any liquid and add the cucumber to the bean sprout mixture. Sprinkle with salt and lemon juice to taste.

Peel and grate the apple or mango and mix with the nuts and coconut. Add to the salad and toss well before serving.

Serves 4

Spinach with Onion and Bacon

2 tablespoons vegetable oil
4 bacon rashers, derinded and
  chopped
1 onion, chopped
1–2 garlic cloves, crushed
500 g (1 lb) spinach leaves
1 tablespoon lemon juice
salt and pepper

Heat the oil in a large pan. Add the bacon, onion and garlic and fry gently for 5 minutes.

Add the spinach and lemon juice and season with salt and pepper to taste. Fry gently for 3–5 minutes, stirring constantly, until the spinach is just tender. Transfer to a serving dish and serve immediately.

Serves 4

far left: spinach with onion and bacon;
left: celery with walnuts

Celery with Walnuts

500 g (1 lb) can celery hearts
25 g (1 oz) butter
25 g (1 oz) walnut pieces

Place the celery hearts, together with their juice, in a saucepan over a moderate heat. When hot, drain, place in a warmed serving dish and keep hot.

Melt the butter in a small pan. Add the walnuts and fry until just beginning to brown. Spoon over the celery and serve immediately.

Serves 4

Spicy Vegetable Medley

3 tablespoons vegetable oil
1 teaspoon fennel seeds
2 onions, sliced
1 teaspoon ground coriander
1 teaspoon cumin seeds
1 teaspoon chilli powder
2 teaspoons chopped fresh root
  ginger
2 garlic cloves, crushed
1 small aubergine, thinly sliced
1 potato, cubed
1 green pepper, cored, deseeded and
  sliced
2 courgettes, sliced
400 g (13 oz) can tomatoes
2 green chillies, chopped
50 g (2 oz) frozen peas
salt

Heat the oil in a pan. Add the fennel seeds and cook, stirring, for 1 minute. Add the onions and cook for 5 minutes until golden brown. Lower the heat, add all the spices and cook for 1 minute. Add the ginger, garlic, aubergine and potato, mix well and cook for 10 minutes.

Add the green pepper, courgettes, tomatoes, together with their juice and chillies and season to taste. Bring to the boil over a low heat, then simmer for 8–10 minutes.

Stir in the peas and cook for 3 minutes. Transfer to a warm serving dish and serve at once.

Serves 4–6

Cheese and Tomato Salad

250 g (8 oz) Saint Paulin cheese
5 tablespoons grapeseed oil
2 tablespoons lemon juice
2 teaspoons chopped parsley
8 leaves basil, finely chopped
4 large ripe firm tomatoes, skinned
   and sliced
8 spring onions, chopped
salt and black pepper
warm crusty bread, to serve
   (optional)
To garnish:
1 lemon, sliced
black olives

Remove and discard the rind and slice the Saint Paulin cheese finely with a serrated knife. Place in a shallow dish.

Beat the oil with the lemon juice, parsley and basil and season with salt and pepper to taste. Pour over the cheese slices, cover and leave to marinate for 30 minutes.

To serve, divide the tomato slices equally among 4 individual serving plates. Top with the cheese and herb mixture and a little spring onion. Garnish with lemon slices and olives.

Serve with warm crusty bread, if liked, to mop up the herby juices.

Serves 4

right: mushroom and emmental salad

Mushroom and Emmental Salad

125 g (4 oz) Emmental cheese
250 g (8 oz) button mushrooms,
   sliced
250 ml (8 fl oz) single cream
juice of 2 lemons
salt and pepper
chopped parsley, to garnish

Cut the Emmental into thin, bite-size strips, place in a bowl and mix thoroughly with the mushrooms and cream.

Add the lemon juice and season with salt and pepper to taste. Toss well to coat.

Spoon the salad into a serving dish, sprinkle with parsley to garnish and serve.

Serves 4

Chicken and Walnut Salad

500 g (1 lb) cooked boned chicken

2 celery sticks, coarsely chopped

1 large dessert apple, cored and diced

50 g (2 oz) walnuts, roughly chopped

6 tablespoons mayonnaise

1–2 tablespoons single cream (optional)

sprigs of watercress, to garnish

Cut the chicken into pieces and place in a large bowl with the celery, apple and walnuts.

Thin the mayonnaise if necessary to give the consistency of thick cream, by adding a little single cream. Pour over the chicken and toss well until the ingredients are evenly coated.

Turn into a serving dish and garnish with watercress.

Serves 4

Artichoke and Bacon Salad

3 tablespoons olive oil
1 tablespoon red or white wine
  vinegar
½ teaspoon wholegrain mustard
½ teaspoon sugar

2 x 400 g (13 oz) cans artichoke
  hearts, drained
50 g (2 oz) lean thick bacon rashers,
  derinded
salt and pepper

Put the oil, vinegar, mustard and sugar in a bowl, season with salt and pepper to taste and whisk the dressing thoroughly.

Add the artichoke hearts to the bowl and toss well in the dressing. Transfer the salad to a serving dish.

Cut the bacon into strips. Place a frying pan over a moderate heat, add the bacon and fry until crisp.

Sprinkle the bacon over the salad and serve immediately.

Serves 4

Melon and Anchovy Salad

1 medium melon
50 g (2 oz) can anchovy fillets
juice of 1 lemon
juice of 1 orange
1 teaspoon caster sugar (optional)
sprigs of watercress, to garnish

Halve the melon and discard the seeds. Scoop the flesh into a serving dish, using a melon baller or cut into cubes. Drain the anchovy fillets, reserving 1 tablespoon of the oil. Cut the anchovies into short slivers and add to the melon.

Mix the lemon and orange juice with the reserved anchovy oil and pour over the salad. Add sugar, if using and chill before serving, garnished with watercress.

Serves 4

Apple, Avocado and Celery Pasta Salad

1 avocado, peeled, pitted and sliced
1 red dessert apple, cored and sliced
2 teaspoons lemon juice
250 g (8 oz) dried pasta shapes (e.g. bows, rings, wheels, shells or twists)
3 tablespoons olive oil
1 tablespoon cider vinegar
½ teaspoon Dijon mustard
½ teaspoon sugar
3 celery sticks, chopped
salt and pepper

Mix the avocado and apple slices with the lemon juice to prevent browning.

Cook the pasta in a pan of boiling salted water for 8–10 minutes until tender, but still firm to the bite. Drain and refresh under cold water.

Put the olive oil, vinegar, mustard and sugar in a screw-top jar, season with salt and pepper to taste and shake vigorously to mix.

Place the cooked pasta, avocado and apple slices, celery and dressing in a serving bowl. Toss gently to mix before serving.

Serves 4

above: melon and anchovy salad;
right: apple, avocado and celery pasta salad

Caesar Bean Salad

500 g (1 lb) can baked beans
juice of ½ lemon
2 teaspoons Worcestershire sauce
2 garlic cloves, crushed
1 egg
5 tablespoons olive oil
2 slices bread, cubed
1 small iceberg lettuce, shredded
1 head chicory, shredded
75 g (3 oz) cooked French beans
12 black olives
salt and pepper
chopped parsley or snipped chives,
   to garnish

Drain the beans thoroughly in a sieve over a bowl. Mix the bean juice with the lemon juice and season with salt and pepper to taste, Worcestershire sauce and half the garlic.

Soft-boil the egg in a pan of boiling water for 45 seconds. Crack the shell carefully and scoop out the liquid egg and add to the dressing. Whisk thoroughly with a fork, adding 2 tablespoons of the oil.

Heat the remaining oil in a shallow pan. Add the remaining garlic and the bread cubes and fry until crisp and golden. Drain on kitchen paper.

Place the lettuce, chicory, French beans and olives in a large serving bowl. Add the drained baked beans and garlic croûtons and mix gently.

Add the prepared dressing and toss gently to mix. Sprinkle with chopped parsley or snipped chives to garnish and serve immediately for a light supper or summer lunch.

Serves 4

Mixed Bean Waldorf Salad

A more traditional Waldorf Salad can be made by omitting the beans and using a creamy dressing, such as mayonnaise blended with some natural yogurt.

500 g (1 lb) can barbecue beans
3 tablespoons olive oil
1 garlic clove, crushed
1 tablespoon chopped mint
3 celery sticks, sliced
125 g (4 oz) French beans

2 tablespoons coarsely chopped walnuts
1 large lettuce heart, quartered
1 red dessert apple, cored and sliced
1 teaspoon lemon juice
salt and pepper

Drain the beans thoroughly in a sieve over a bowl. Mix the bean juice with the oil, salt and pepper to taste, garlic and half of the chopped mint, blending well.

Mix the drained barbecue beans with the celery, French beans, half of the walnuts and a little of the prepared dressing.

Arrange the lettuce heart on a serving dish. Toss the apple slices in the lemon juice to prevent discoloration and arrange around the lettuce.

Spoon the barbecue bean mixture on top of the lettuce and spoon over the remaining dressing. Sprinkle with the remaining walnuts and mint. Keep cool until ready to serve or serve immediately.

Serves 4

left: caesar bean salad;
above: *mixed bean waldorf salad*

Beetroot and Orange Salad

2 large oranges
3 tablespoons olive oil
1 tablespoon orange juice
½ teaspoon French mustard
½ teaspoon sugar
1 garlic clove, finely sliced (optional)
500 g (1 lb) cooked beetroot, sliced
sprigs of watercress or mint, to
  garnish

Grate the rind from 1 of the oranges. Mix together the olive oil, orange juice, mustard, sugar, garlic, if using, and orange rind in a screw-top jar and shake vigorously to mix. Peel and thinly slice both oranges, removing all pith.

Arrange the orange and beetroot slices in alternate layers in a serving dish. Pour the dressing over the top and garnish with watercress or mint sprigs. Chill before serving.

Serves 4

Date and Nut Salad

175 g (6 oz) dates, pitted and halved
3 crisp dessert apples, cored and
  sliced
50 g (2 oz) walnut pieces
3 tablespoons lemon juice
150 ml (¼ pint) natural yogurt
salt

Put the dates, apples and walnuts in a serving bowl.

Mix together the lemon juice and yogurt. Add salt to taste. Pour over the salad and toss well until the ingredients are evenly coated.

Serves 4

above: beetroot and orange salad;
left: date and nut salad;
right: carrot and raisin salad

Carrot and Raisin Salad

Soy sauce is indispensable in Asian cooking. It is used as a seasoning, marinade, dressing or to colour dished. Light soy sauce is generally used with vegetables, dipping sauces, chicken, seafood and soup.

500 g (1 lb) carrots
75 g (3 oz) raisins or sultanas
2 tablespoons soy sauce
chopped parsley or coriander,
    to garnish

Peel and grate the carrots and place them in a large serving bowl. Add the raisins or sultanas and mix thoroughly. Sprinkle over the soy sauce and toss well. Garnish with chopped parsley or coriander.

Serves 4

Note: As a tasty and colourful variation, replace half of the carrots with coarsely grated white cabbage or celery. You could also substitute the soy sauce with a rice vinegar, if liked.

Avocado with Pears and Olives

2 avocados
2 tablespoons lemon juice
6 large black olives
4½ teaspoons mayonnaise
200 g (7 oz) can pear quarters,
   drained and diced
salt and pepper

Halve the avocados, discard the stones and rub the cut surfaces of the avocados with a little of the lemon juice to prevent them from discolouring.

Halve the olives and discard the stones. Set aside 4 halves for garnish and chop the remainder.

Mix the mayonnaise and remaining lemon juice together in a bowl. Add the diced pears and chopped olives and season with salt and pepper to taste. Mix well.

Divide the mixture among the avocado halves. Garnish each portion with an olive half and serve immediately.

Serves 4

above: avocado with pears and olives;
top right: *tomatoes with horseradish mayonnaise;*
bottom right: *corn fritters*

Tomatoes with Horseradish Mayonnaise

4 large tomatoes, sliced
3 tablespoons mayonnaise
1 tablespoon creamed horseradish
1–2 tablespoons single cream (optional)
chopped parsley, to garnish

Arrange the sliced tomatoes in a serving dish. Mix the mayonnaise with the horseradish, adding a little of the single cream if necessary to give the dressing the consistency of thick cream.

Spoon the dressing over the tomatoes and garnish with a sprinkling of parsley.

Serves 4

Corn Fritters

325 g (11 oz) can sweetcorn kernels, drained
2 teaspoons soft brown sugar
3 eggs, beaten
50 g (2 oz) butter, melted
4 tablespoons grated Parmesan cheese
oil, for deep-frying
salt and pepper
sprigs of watercress, to garnish

Put the sweetcorn in a bowl. Add the sugar, eggs, butter and cheese and season to taste. Mix thoroughly.

Heat the oil in a deep-fat fryer to 180–190°C (350–375°F) or until a cube of bread browns in 30 seconds. Drop spoonfuls of the corn mixture into the oil and fry for 4 minutes.

Remove and drain on kitchen paper and serve warm, garnished with watercress.

Serves 4

Mushroom and Onion Casserole

50 g (2 oz) butter
500 g (1 lb) onions, roughly chopped
500 g (1 lb) mushrooms, sliced
200 ml (7 fl oz) stock
2 tablespoons sherry
2 tablespoons lemon juice
salt and pepper
chopped parsley, to garnish

Melt the butter in a flameproof casserole. Add the onions and fry gently for 10 minutes, until softened. Add the mushrooms, stock, sherry and lemon juice and season with salt and pepper to taste.

Cover and cook in a preheated oven, 180°C (350°F), Gas Mark 4, for 15 minutes. Serve hot, garnished with parsley.

Serves 4

Herb Glazed Carrots

500 g (1 lb) can baby carrots
25 g (1 oz) butter
2 teaspoons sugar
6 mint leaves, finely chopped

Put the carrots, together with their juice, in a saucepan and place over a moderate heat. When they are hot, drain well.

Place the butter and sugar in a small pan. Heat gently, stirring, until dissolved, then add the mint. Add the carrots and toss well.

Turn into a warmed serving dish. Serve hot.

Serves 4

Baked Onions

8 medium onions, unpeeled
salt and pepper
chopped parsley, to garnish

Cut a small piece off the root end of each onion. Cut off the tops and make 4 vertical slits through the skin from the top to the middle of each onion.

Place on a baking sheet and cook in a preheated oven, 180°C (350°F), Gas Mark 4, for 25–30 minutes until the centres are tender.

Remove the skins from the onions. Season with salt and pepper to taste and garnish with parsley. Serve hot.

Serves 4

right from the top: mushroom and onion casserole; herb glazed carrots; baked onions

Braised Cabbage with Bacon

2 rashers back bacon, derinded and
   chopped
1 small white cabbage, roughly
   chopped
1 onion, chopped
6 tablespoons natural yogurt
6 tablespoons chicken stock
1 teaspoon paprika
salt and pepper

Place a frying pan over a moderate
heat. Add the bacon and cook
briskly until crisp. Transfer to an
ovenproof dish and add the cabbage
and onion.

Mix the yogurt, stock and paprika
together and season with salt and
pepper to taste. Pour over the
cabbage.

Cover and cook in a preheated
oven, 200°C (400°F), Gas Mark 6,
for 25–30 minutes, stirring halfway
through cooking. Transfer to a
warmed serving dish and serve hot.

Serves 4

Brussels Sprouts with Chestnuts

125 g (4 oz) chestnuts
500 g (1 lb) frozen Brussels sprouts
25 g (1 oz) butter
salt

Score the chestnuts around the
middle and place on a baking sheet.
Bake in a preheated oven, 180°C
(350°F), Gas Mark 4, for 10 minutes.
When cool enough to handle, peel
the chestnuts.

Cook the sprouts in a saucepan of
boiling, lightly salted water for
about 3–5 minutes.

Meanwhile, melt the butter in a
shallow pan. Add the chestnuts and
fry briskly, turning, for 2 minutes.

Drain the sprouts and place in a
serving dish. Add the chestnuts and
butter. Serve immediately.

Serves 4

Italian Cauliflower Salad

1 cauliflower, broken into florets
5 tablespoons olive oil
1½ tablespoons wine vinegar
1 tablespoon capers, drained
1 tablespoon chopped parsley
a few black olives
50 g (2 oz) anchovy fillets, drained
   and sliced
salt and pepper

Put the cauliflower into a saucepan
of boiling, lightly salted water and
cook until tender but still firm,
about 5–6 minutes. Drain and rinse
under cold running water.

Mix the oil, vinegar and a little
salt and pepper together in a salad
bowl. Add the cauliflower and toss
gently. Sprinkle with the capers,
parsley and olives. Arrange the
anchovy fillets in a lattice pattern
on top. Serve immediately.

Serves 4

top left: braised cabbage with bacon;
bottom left: brussels sprouts with
chestnuts

Desserts

Stuffed Oranges

2 large oranges
1 dessert apple, peeled, cored and
   chopped
1 tablespoon raisins
1 tablespoon chopped dates
1 tablespoon hazelnuts, toasted and
   chopped
1 tablespoon soft brown sugar
125 ml (4 fl oz) double cream
1 teaspoon icing sugar
orange twists, to decorate (optional)

Halve the oranges and scoop out
the flesh, keeping the shells intact.
Set the shells aside.

Chop the orange flesh, discarding
all the pith, and place in a bowl.
Add the apple, raisins, dates, nuts
and brown sugar. Mix well and pile
into the orange halves.

Whip the cream with the icing
sugar until it forms soft peaks.
Spoon on top of the filled oranges.
Chill before serving, decorated with
orange twists, if liked.

Serves 4

Citrus Trifles

4 trifle sponges
2 tablespoons Cointreau
2 oranges
3 tablespoons lemon curd
2 egg whites
4 lemon twists, to decorate

Place the trifle sponges into
4 individual glass dishes and
sprinkle with the Cointreau.

Peel the oranges, removing all
pith, and chop the flesh roughly.
Divide the oranges between the
trifle dishes.

Put the lemon curd in a bowl.
Whisk the egg whites until stiff and
fold them into the lemon curd.
Spoon the lemon mixture over the
orange segments.

Decorate with lemon twists. Chill
before serving.

Serves 4

Apple Toffee Dessert

1 cooking apple, peeled, cored and
   chopped
1 large dessert apple, peeled, cored
   and chopped
50 g (2 oz) demerara or soft brown
   sugar
50 g (2 oz) butter
juice of ½ lemon
2 slices day old white bread, crusts
   removed, cut into cubes
4 tablespoons double cream, lightly
   whipped, to serve

Sprinkle the apples with the sugar
and toss well to coat evenly.

Melt half the butter in a frying
pan, add the apples and fry quickly
until just soft. Transfer to a warm
serving dish, using a slotted spoon.
Sprinkle with the lemon juice and
keep warm.

Melt the remaining butter in the
pan, add the bread cubes and fry,
turning, until crisp and evenly
golden.

Add the bread to the apple and
mix well. Serve immediately, topped
with whipped cream.

Serves 4

Treacle Tart

250 g (8 oz) packet shortcrust pastry, defrosted, if frozen
4 tablespoons cornflakes, crushed, or fresh white breadcrumbs
6 tablespoons golden syrup, warmed
juice of ½ lemon
½ teaspoon ground ginger

Roll out the pastry and use to line a 20 cm (8 inch) ovenproof plate. Trim, knock up the edge and flute. Reserve the pastry trimmings. Prick the pastry base.

Sprinkle half the cornflakes or breadcrumbs in the pastry case and pour in the syrup. Sprinkle the lemon juice over the syrup.

Mix the ginger with the remaining cornflakes or breadcrumbs and sprinkle over the syrup and lemon juice mixture. Cut strips from the pastry trimmings and make a lattice pattern over the treacle tart.

Cook in a preheated oven, 190°C (375°F), Gas Mark 5, for 25 minutes until the pastry is crisp and golden. Serve hot or cold, with cream.

Serves 4

Fudge Brownies

125 g (4 oz) butter or margarine, softened, plus extra for greasing
250 g (8 oz) dark soft brown sugar
1 teaspoon vanilla essence
2 eggs, beaten
50 g (2 oz) plain flour
25 g (1 oz) cocoa powder
½ teaspoon baking powder
125 g (4 oz) walnuts, chopped
1 tablespoon milk

Topping and decoration:
125 g (4 oz) plain chocolate, broken into pieces
15 g (½ oz) butter
125 g (4 oz) icing sugar, sifted
2 tablespoons warm water
12 walnut halves

Grease an 18 x 28 cm (7 x 11 inch) oblong cake tin and line the base with greased greaseproof paper.

In a bowl beat the butter or margarine with the sugar and vanilla essence until soft and creamy. Gradually add the eggs, beating well after each addition.

Sift the flour with the cocoa and baking powder on to the creamed mixture, add the walnuts and milk and fold in gently but thoroughly, using a large metal spoon. Turn the mixture into the prepared tin and smooth the surface.

Bake in a preheated oven, 180°C (350°F), Gas Mark 4, for 25 minutes until well risen and cooked through. Turn on to a wire rack and leave to cool.

Melt the chocolate and butter, without stirring, in a heatproof bowl set over a saucepan of hot, but not boiling, water. Remove from the heat and gradually stir in the icing sugar and water to make a thick coating consistency. Use the chocolate topping at once, spooned evenly over the cooked cake and swirled with a knife.

Cut into 12 squares and decorate each with a walnut half.

Makes 12

Coffee-flavoured Chocolate Mousse

175 g (6 oz) plain chocolate, broken into pieces
3 tablespoons strong black coffee
1 tablespoon brandy

4 eggs, separated
To decorate:
150 ml (¼ pint) double cream, whipped
flaked almonds, toasted

Put the chocolate, coffee and brandy in a bowl over a saucepan of hot water. Stir until the chocolate is melted. Remove from the heat and leave to cool for 1 minute.

Beat in the egg yolks to the chocolate mixture. Whisk the egg whites until stiff and fold into the mixture. Pour into a soufflé dish and chill before serving. Decorate with whipped cream and almonds.

Serves 4

*left: treacle tart; **above:** coffee-flavoured chocolate mousse*

Butterscotch Nut Pie

25 g (1 oz) butter
6 digestive biscuits, crushed
200 ml (7 fl oz) milk
125 ml (4 fl oz) single cream
1 x 75 g (3 oz) packet butterscotch
    instant dessert
50 g (2 oz) hazelnuts, toasted and
    chopped
To decorate:
150 ml (¼ pint) double cream,
    whipped
hazelnuts, toasted

Melt the butter and stir in the
biscuit crumbs. Press into the base
of a 15 cm (6 inch) flan dish.

Gradually add the milk and cream
to the butterscotch dessert, mixing
until smooth. Add the hazelnuts
and pile on top of the biscuit base.

Decorate with whipped cream
and hazelnuts just before serving.

Serves 4

Chocolate Nut Curls

75 g (3 oz) butter or margarine, plus
    extra for greasing
75 g (3 oz) caster sugar
40 g (1½ oz) plain flour, sifted
15 g (½ oz) cocoa powder, sifted
50 g (2 oz) hazelnuts, chopped

Grease 2 or more baking sheets and
set aside.

Cream the butter or margarine
and sugar together until light and
fluffy. Stir in the flour, cocoa and
hazelnuts and mix well.

Place 4 teaspoonfuls of the
mixture well apart on each of the
baking sheets and flatten with a
dampened fork.

Bake in a preheated oven, 200°C
(400°F), Gas Mark 6, for about
6–8 minutes until pale golden.

Leave on the baking sheets for
1 minute, then remove with a
palette knife and place on a rolling
pin to curl. Leave until set, then
remove very carefully.

Bake and curl the remaining
mixture in the same way.

Makes 20–24

Coffee Parfait

3 teaspoons instant coffee powder
1 teaspoon drinking chocolate
    powder
2 teaspoons boiling water
¼ teaspoon vanilla essence
300 ml (½ pint) whipping cream
2 egg whites
50 g (2 oz) caster sugar
40 g (1½ oz) plain chocolate, grated
almond biscuits, to serve (optional)

Dissolve the coffee and drinking
chocolate powder in the boiling
water, then leave to cool. Add the
vanilla essence.

Whisk the cream until stiff and
fold in the coffee and chocolate
mixture, using a metal spoon.

Whisk the egg whites stiffly, then
gradually add the sugar, whisking
well after each addition until very
stiff and glossy.

Lightly fold the egg whites and
25 g (1 oz) of the grated chocolate
into the cream mixture, using a
metal spoon.

Spoon the mixture into 6 serving
dishes, sprinkle with the remaining
grated chocolate and serve chilled,
with almond biscuits, if liked.

Serves 6

left: butterscotch nut pie

Crunchy Rhubarb Flans

50 g (2 oz) butter, melted

200 g (7 oz) coconut biscuits, finely crushed

300 g (10 oz) rhubarb, cut into 2.5 cm (1 inch) lengths

2 tablespoons orange juice

75 g (3 oz) caster sugar

2 tablespoons cornflour

1 egg, separated

4 orange twists, to decorate

Combine the butter and biscuit crumbs and divide the mixture between 4 individual 10 cm (4 inch) flan dishes, pressing over the bases and up the sides.

Put the rhubarb, orange juice and sugar into a saucepan, bring to the boil, then cover and simmer for 4 minutes, or until tender. Process in a blender or food processor until smooth or rub through a sieve.

Put the cornflour into a saucepan and stir in a little rhubarb purée. Add the remaining purée and the egg yolk, bring to the boil, stirring, then simmer for 1 minute.

Whisk the egg white until stiff, then fold into the rhubarb mixture. Spoon into the flan cases.

Bake in a preheated oven, 200°C (400°F), Gas Mark 6, for about 8–10 minutes or until set.

Serve hot or cold, decorated with a twist of orange.

Serves 4

Yogurt Cheesecake

175 g (6 oz) cream cheese

150 ml (¼ pint) natural yogurt

2 drops vanilla essence

2 tablespoons thick honey

2 teaspoons lemon juice

1 x 15–18 cm (6–7 inch) sponge flan ring

125 g (4 oz) frozen blackberries, defrosted

Beat the cheese and yogurt together until smooth. Add the vanilla essence, honey and lemon juice and beat until thoroughly blended.

Spoon the cream mixture into the flan case and top with the blackberries. Chill before serving.

Serves 4

Moroccan Orange Salad

4 large or 6 medium oranges

50 g (2 oz) dates, roughly chopped

25 g (1 oz) flaked almonds

2 tablespoons caster sugar

juice of 2 lemons

ground cinnamon, to decorate

double cream, to serve (optional)

Peel and slice the oranges, discarding the pith. Place the slices in a serving dish, together with the dates and almonds.

Mix together the sugar and lemon juice and pour over the fruit mixture. Chill before serving.

Sprinkle with cinnamon to taste. Serve with cream, if liked

Serves 4

right: yogurt cheesecake;
far right: moroccan orange salad

Ginger Rum Trifle

250 g (8 oz) ginger cake, sliced

250 g (8 oz) can pear quarters

6 tablespoons rum

300 ml (½ pint) cold thick custard

150 ml (¼ pint) double cream

1–2 teaspoons icing sugar

flaked almonds, toasted, to decorate

Line a soufflé dish or bowl with half the ginger cake. Drain the pears, reserving 2 tablespoons of the juice. Mix the rum with the pear juice and sprinkle half over the cake. Place the pears on top, cover with the remaining cake and pour over the remaining rum mixture.

Spoon the custard over the cake. Whip the cream with the sugar until it forms peaks, spoon over the custard; decorate with almonds.

Serves 4

Caledonian Cream

3 tablespoons ginger marmalade

250 ml (8 fl oz) double cream

3 tablespoon caster sugar

2 tablespoons whisky

2 tablespoons lemon juice

2 egg whites

soft brown or demerara sugar, to decorate

Divide the marmalade between 4 individual glass dishes.

Whip the cream until stiff, then fold in the caster sugar, whisky and lemon juice. Whisk the egg whites until stiff and fold into the cream mixture.

Spoon the cream mixture over the marmalade and sprinkle with brown sugar to decorate.

Serves 4

Lemon Cream Swiss Roll

75 g (3 oz) soft margarine, plus extra for greasing

200 g (7 oz) caster sugar

3 eggs

175 g (6 oz) self-raising flour, sifted

½ teaspoon finely grated lemon rind

150 ml (¼ pint) whipping cream

2 tablespoons lemon curd

1 tablespoon toasted, chopped mixed nuts (optional)

1 tablespoon icing sugar, sifted, for dredging

Grease a 33 x 23 cm (13 x 9 inch) Swiss roll tin and line the base and sides with greaseproof paper.

Put the margarine, 175 g (6 oz) of the sugar, the eggs, flour and lemon rind in a large mixing bowl and beat well with a wooden spoon for 2-3 minutes, or with an electric mixer for 1 minute.

Turn the mixture into the prepared Swiss roll tin and spread out evenly. Bake in a preheated oven, 190°C (375°F), Gas Mark 5, for 12–15 minutes or until well risen, light golden and cooked through. To test, press lightly in the centre with the little finger. If the sponge springs back it is done; if your finger leaves an impression, bake for a further few minutes.

Meanwhile, have ready on a work surface a large sheet of greaseproof paper, placed over a dampened tea towel. Dredge the greaseproof paper evenly with the remaining sugar.

Turn the sponge out on to the sugared paper. Quickly, but carefully, remove the lining paper and trim the edges neatly.

Working quickly, roll up the Swiss roll, starting with the short end and using the greaseproof paper to help you form a neat roll. Wrap closely in the greaseproof paper to hold the roll in shape and leave to cool.

Whip the cream until soft peaks form, then add the lemon curd and whisk again until thick and mixed.

Unroll the Swiss roll and spread evenly with the lemon cream mixture. Sprinkle with chopped nuts, if using, and re-roll neatly. Sprinkle over the top with icing sugar and serve the Swiss Roll cut into chunky slices.

Serves 4

far left: ginger rum trifle;
left: caledonian cream

Soufflé Flambé

butter, for greasing
6 eggs, separated, plus 2 egg whites
125 g (4 oz) caster sugar, plus extra,
    for sprinkling
1 teaspoon vanilla essence
1–2 tablespoons Grand Marnier

Grease a large ovenproof dish with butter and sprinkle with sugar. Beat the egg yolks with the sugar and vanilla essence until light and smooth.

Beat the egg whites until they are very stiff, then fold into them the yolk and sugar mixture. The mixture should be very light.

Pour the soufflé mixture into the prepared dish and bake in a preheated oven, 200°C (400°F), Gas Mark 6, for about 10–12 minutes until it is risen and golden.

Warm the Grand Marnier in a ladle at the table. Pour in over the soufflé, ignite it and serve the soufflé immediately.

Serves 4

Pears en Compôte

500 g (1 lb) can pear halves
300 ml (½ pint) red wine
2 teaspoons ground cinnamon
50 g (2 oz) dates, chopped
double cream, to serve (optional)

Drain the pears, reserving 150 ml (¼ pint) of the juice. Place the pears, wine, reserved pear juice and cinnamon in a pan. Bring to the boil, then lower the heat, cover and simmer for 10 minutes.

Add the dates, remove from the heat and leave to cool. Serve chilled, with cream, if liked.

Serves 4

Baked Bananas

50 g (2 oz) butter
2 tablespoons soft brown sugar
2 tablespoons lemon juice
4 bananas
2 tablespoons brandy
single cream, to serve

Put the butter, sugar and lemon juice in a shallow casserole. Place in a preheated oven, 180°C (350°F), Gas Mark 4, for a few minutes until melted.

Cut the bananas into large pieces and arrange in the casserole, turning to coat with the sauce. Add the brandy, cover and return to the oven for 25 minutes.

Serve piping hot, accompanied by single cream.

Serves 4

right: pears en compôte;
far right: baked bananas

Port and Prune Fool

300 ml (½ pint) double cream
475 g (15 oz) can prunes, pitted
4 tablespoons port
50 g (2 oz) soft brown sugar
grated nutmeg
chopped nuts, to decorate

Whip the cream until stiff. Chop the prunes and fold into the cream with the port, sugar and nutmeg to taste.

Spoon into individual glass dishes and chill. Decorate with chopped nuts before serving.

Serves 4

Ginger Log

24 ginger snaps
4 tablespoons rum
450 ml (¾ pint) double cream
1½ teaspoons ground ginger
4½ teaspoons caster sugar
4½ teaspoons ginger syrup (from stem ginger)
stem ginger slices, to decorate

Place the biscuits in a shallow dish and sprinkle with the rum. Leave until completely absorbed.

Whip the cream with the ground ginger and sugar until stiff. Fold in the ginger syrup.

Sandwich all the biscuits together, using two-thirds of the cream mixture, to make a long roll. Place on a serving dish and cover with the remaining cream. Decorate with the stem ginger.

Serves 4

Mont Blanc Meringues

125 ml (4 fl oz) double cream
250 g (8 oz) can sweetened chestnut purée
2 tablespoons Grand Marnier
8 meringue nests
flaked almonds, toasted, to decorate

Whip the cream until stiff, then fold half into the chestnut purée, together with the Grand Marnier.

Pile the chestnut cream into the meringue nests. Swirl the remaining cream on top so that the filling resembles a snow-capped peak.

Decorate with almonds and serve immediately.

Serves 4

left (clockwise from the top): port and prune fool; ginger log; mont blanc meringues

Hawaiian Fritters

250 g (8 oz) can pineapple slices, drained, with juice reserved
2 tablespoons golden syrup
vegetable oil, for deep-frying
75 g (3 oz) plain flour
3 teaspoons vegetable oil
125 ml (4 fl oz) water
2 tablespoons desiccated coconut
1 egg white
2 medium bananas, peeled and cut into chunks
ice cream, to serve

Pat the pineapple slices dry on absorbent paper. Place the pineapple juice and golden syrup in a saucepan, bring to the boil and boil gently for 10 minutes.

Meanwhile heat the oil for deep frying to 180–190°C (350–375°F) or until a cube of bread browns in 30 seconds.

Sift the flour into a bowl. Mix together the oil and water and add to the flour. Mix well to form a smooth batter. Stir in the coconut.

Whisk the egg white until stiff and gently fold into the batter, using a large metal spoon. Dip the pineapple slices and banana chunks into the batter and fry in the hot oil for about 6 minutes, or until golden brown and heated through. Drain on absorbent kitchen paper.

Arrange the fritters on a warm serving plate and spoon over the hot syrup. Serve hot with ice cream.

Serves 4

Ginger and Fruit Salad

2 apples, cored, but not peeled
2 apricots, peeled
1 orange, peeled
250 ml (8 fl oz) ginger ale
2 bananas
2 tablespoons lemon juice
50 g (2 oz) seedless green grapes

Dice the apples and apricots. Remove the pith from the orange and divide the flesh into segments.

Mix the apples, apricots and orange together in a bowl and pour over the ginger ale. Slice the bananas and mix with the lemon juice and grapes. Add to the bowl. Mix all the fruit and juices together thoroughly. Serve the salad from a serving dish or in individual glasses.

Serves 4

Grape Jelly

15 g (½ oz) powdered gelatine
150 ml (¼ pint) boiling water
450 ml (¾ pint) unsweetened grape juice
green colouring
250 g (8 oz) green grapes, peeled
250 g (8 oz) cottage cheese
300 ml (½ pint) natural yogurt

Dissolve the gelatine in the water and add the grape juice, with a few drops of colouring. Pour into 6 tall glasses. Divide the grapes between the glasses, reserving a few to decorate, and leave tilted in a cool place to set.

Sieve the cottage cheese or process in a blender or food processor until smooth. Fold in the yogurt and spoon the mixture over the jelly. Decorate with the reserved grapes. Chill before serving.

Serves 6

right: ginger and fruit salad;
far right: grape jelly

Peaches and Cream Flan

15 g (½ oz) butter
125 g (4 oz) digestive biscuits, finely
  crushed
400 g (13 oz) can peach slices,
  drained
300 ml (½ pint) soured cream
25 g (1 oz) caster sugar
a little freshly grated nutmeg
  (optional)
150 ml (¼ pint) whipping cream,
  whipped, to decorate

Grease a 23 cm (9 inch) ovenproof
flan dish with the butter. Press the
biscuit crumbs into the base of the
flan dish.

Put the peach slices, soured cream
and sugar into a food processor or
blender and process for 30 seconds
until the mixture is smooth and
thoroughly combined.

Pour the mixture into the flan
case, smooth the surface and
sprinkle with nutmeg, if using. Bake
in a preheated oven, 180°C (350°F),
Gas Mark 4, for 25–30 minutes.

Leave to cool, then chill before
serving, decorated with cream.

Serves 6

Orange Pots

3 tablespoons orange juice
4 teaspoons lemon juice
4 teaspoons powdered gelatine
375 g (12 oz) cottage cheese
6 tablespoons buttermilk
1–2 tablespoons caster sugar
1 orange, thinly sliced, to decorate

Put the orange and lemon juice in a
small bowl and sprinkle the gelatine
over the top. Stand over a bowl of
hot, but not boiling, water to
dissolve the gelatine.

Put the orange gelatine into a
blender or food processor, together
with the cottage cheese, buttermilk
and sugar to taste and process until
it is smooth.

Divide the mixture between
4 dessert glasses and decorate with
quartered slices of orange.

Serves 4

Rhubarb Fool

500 g (1 lb) rhubarb, cut into 5 cm
  (2 inch) lengths
2 tablespoons lemon juice
finely grated rind of ½ lemon
50 g (2 oz) caster sugar
3 tablespoons water
2 egg yolks
150 ml (¼ pint) natural yogurt

Put the rhubarb into a saucepan
with the lemon juice, grated lemon
rind, sugar and water. Simmer over
a low heat until tender.

Rub through a sieve or process in
a blender or food processor. When
cool, beat in the egg yolks and fold
in the yogurt so that the fool is
streaked with threads of rhubarb.
Spoon into small dishes and chill
before serving.

Serves 4

right: orange pots;
far right: rhubarb fool

Index